THE DECORATION OF HOUSES

THE CLASSICAL AMERICA SERIES
IN ART AND ARCHITECTURE

Henry Hope Reed and H. Stafford Bryant, Jr., General Editors

The American Vignola by William R. Ware
The Architecture of Humanism by Geoffrey Scott
The Classic Point of View by Kenyon Cox
The Decoration of Houses by Edith Wharton and Ogden Codman, Jr.
The Golden City by Henry Hope Reed
The Library of Congress by Herbert Small
The New York Public Library by Henry Hope Reed
Fragments from Greek and Roman Architecture
    The Classical America Edition of Hector d'Espouy's Plates
Man as Hero: The Human Figure in Art by Pierce Rice
    (in preparation)
Monumental Classic Architecture in Great Britain and Ireland
    by Albert E. Richardson

THE CLASSICAL AMERICA PERIODICAL
    Classical America IV, edited by William A. Coles

With the Architectural Book Publishing Company

Student's Edition of the *Monograph of the Work of McKim,*
    Mead & White, 1879–1915
Student's Edition of *Paul Letarouilly's Buildings of Renaissance*
    Rome (in preparation)

Classical America is the society which encourages the classical tradition in the arts of the United States. Inquiries about the society should be sent to Classical America, in care of W. W. Norton & Company, Inc., 500 Fifth Avenue, New York, N.Y. 10110.

This edition of *The American Vignola* is being published under a grant from Arthur Ross to Classical America. Classical America is a society founded to promote the classical tradition in the arts of the United States.

THE DECORATION OF HOUSES

Edith Wharton and Ogden Codman, Jr.

Introductory Notes by John Barrington Bayley and William A. Coles

W · W · NORTON & COMPANY

New York · London

W. W. Norton & Company, Inc., 500 Fifth Avenue, New York, N.Y. 10110
W. W. Norton & Company Ltd., 37 Great Russell Street, London WC1B 3NU

Copyright © 1978 by W. W. Norton & Company, Inc.
Published simultaneously in Canada by
Penguin Books Canada Ltd,
2801 John Street, Markham, Ontario L3R 1B4.
Printed in the United States of America.

This edition first published by W. W. Norton & Company, Inc. 1978
by arrangement with Classical America, as part of the Classical
America Series in Art and Architecture.

NOTE: Plates III, VI, VII, VIII, X, XI, XII, XIII, XIV, XV, XVI, XVII, XX, XXI, XXV, XXVII, XXIX, XXXV, XXXVIII, XL, XLIII, XLIV, XLVIII, XLVIII, XLIX, LII, LIII, LIV, and LV are new photographs, which replace originals in the text. In those cases where the photograph is not an exact duplicate of the original illustration the caption has been altered accordingly.

Library of Congress Cataloging in Publication Data
Wharton, Edith Newbold Jones, 1862-1937.
The decoration of houses.
(The Classical America series in art and architecture)
Reprint of the 1902 ed. published by Scribner, New
York; with additional material.
1. Interior decoration. I. Codman, Ogden, joint
author. II. Title. III. Series
[NK2110.W5   1978]   747'.8'8   78-17020

ISBN 0-393-04468-8

ISBN 0-393-00840-1 pbk.

4 5 6 7 8 9 0

Contents

ACKNOWLEDGMENTS

The general editors would like especially to thank the following for their assistance with illustrations and other editorial aspects of reprinting this book: Alfred Branam, Jr., Suzanne R. Boorsch and James Parker of the Metropolitan Museum of Art; Janet L. Snow of Art Reference Bureau, Jerome Zerbe, Michael George, Pierce Rice, Allyn Cox, Charles G. K. Warner, Mr. Bayley, and Mr. Coles. Mr. Coles would like to indicate special debt to Curtis and Barbara Chapin and to R. W. B. Lewis's *Edith Wharton*, which is now the standard biography of the author. Particular thanks are due to Michelle Cliff for expert and manifold editorial assistance.

THE DECORATION OF HOUSES AS A PRACTICAL HANDBOOK
BY JOHN BARRINGTON BAYLEY

This book has charm. Somehow the *douceur de vivre* of the Franco-American life style, which is our very best, comes through on these pages. *The Decoration of Houses* brings to mind the pictures of Walter Gay: There are the reflections in looking-glasses, and on parquet, and the garnitures of chimney-pieces, *boiseries,* the odor of wax; outside the tall glazed doors there is a sunny silent terrace, we are now at Mrs. Wharton's Pavillon Colombe—a well laid out parterre, a rose garden, and an orchard of Reinette apples and luscious double cherries (all of which survive). Again, here is the *douceur de vivre* of the calm, well-ordered house, the life of *juste milieu* where delicious meals are served on time and no guest stays too long, where there are *suitable*—a key word in this book—rooms for different hours and occupations. *"Sic situ laentantur Lares"*—The household gods delight in being here.

The world is not to be reinvented. *Suitability* as used in this book is rooted in the traditions of the Graeco-Roman world. (I am reminded as I write this that the sources for *The Decoration of Houses*

vii

WALTER GAY'S *THE COMMODE,* PAINTED FROM
HIS CHATEAU DU BRÉAU, SEINE-ET-MARNE,
FRANCE

are not solely French: many examples come from Italian interiors of the Renaissance and Baroque periods, and there are a few views of the grander rooms from the English Georgian period.)

As president of Classical America, I take a decidedly partisan view: tradition lays down the ground rules, and they are an expression of what life is all about. One of civilization's tasks is to find rituals which give human existence significance. The rites of daily life are ritualized by *suitable* rooms, *le decor de la vie.* They must be classical rooms because classical architecture is the only architecture that expresses human dignity and greatness. The classical house is a prefiguration of a society which affirms a hierarchy of values. These are the ground rules. All of this is, of course, quite opposed to the contemporary odyssey of the self-centered self.

When Edith Wharton and Ogden Codman wrote *The Decoration of Houses,* lambrequins with passementerie and tassels adorned curtains which hung over lace curtains covering plate-glass windows in one-over-one sash. Tables displayed little gilded easels for photographs and albums with heavy clasps. Polar bear pelts lay on yellow varnished parquet. Oriental rugs were spread upon deep-tufted sofas. Pseudo-Renaissance bronze or gilt candelabra with touches of porcelain flanked matching clocks. Dried pampas grass and thistles stood in cloisonné jars, and there were palms and more palms in giant Satsuma jardinières. On the walls, papered in gaudy colors or paneled with gilt moulding strips, were autographed fans and cases of embroidered velvet which held visiting cards, and over these, glazed pictures climbed to the cornice.

Today's specimen room is a little museum. It has white walls and touches every cultural base: a Congo paddle, Bénin, Grosz, Navajo, a Baroque drawing, Tiffany glass, mobiles, abstracts, Op, Pop, Porn, Eames, Bauhaus.

Both rooms are nonarchitectural, but the first is awash with ornamental objects, the second is clinical with specimens on display. We have been on a starvation diet as to ornament for a good long time; now, with the demise of modern art, a strong reaction —the swing of the pendulum—for ornament is upon us. To be sure, there is a certain amount of confusion in this rage for ornament, because the rage is not necessarily for proper *classical* architectural ornament. I have heard the words "figure sculpture, symmetry, and ornament" being put forward as the basis for a new classicism. This could be a recipe for Angkor Wat and Hindu temples with the daughters of Mara going into their dance.

The ornament of classical architecture is most surely somewhere else, being based on the Greek orders (and their Roman developments) and the proportions which derive from them. Edith Wharton and Ogden Codman on the subject of ornament:

> The attempt to remedy this deficiency in some slight degree has made it necessary to dwell at length upon the strictly architectural principles which controlled the work of the old decorators. The effects that they aimed at having been based mainly on the due adjustment of parts, it has been impossible to explain their methods without assuming their standpoint—that of *architectural proportion*—in contradistinction to the modern view of house-decoration as *superficial application of ornament.*

Unfortunately, it is usually by ornamental details, rather than by proportion, that people distinguish one style from another. This exaggerated estimate of the importance of detail is very characteristic of an imperfect culture . . . [i.e., the confused and turgid ornament of the Early Renaissance in France and Britain.] In other words, decoration is always subservient to proportion; and a room, whatever its decoration may be, must represent the style to which its proportions belong. The less cannot include the greater.

To conform to a style, then, is to accept those rules of proportion which the artistic experience of centuries has established as the best . . .

Proportion is the good breeding of architecture. It is that something, indefinable to the unprofessional eye, which gives repose and distinction to a room . . . in its effects as intangible as that all-pervading essence which the ancients called the soul.

These precepts, however noble, are somewhat ineffable. What follows is down to earth, and is, I think, the finest thing in the book:

. . . the interior walls are invariably treated as an order.

In well-finished rooms the order is usually imagined as resting, not on the floor, but on pedestals, or rather on a continuous pedestal. This continuous pedestal, or "dado" as it is usually called, is represented by a plinth surmounted by mouldings.

In another recent Classical America reprint, *The American Vignola*, there is an important correlative text (in the caption to Plate XVI, "Pedestals and Pilasters"). And it gives a clear idea of this important rule that the interior wall is an Order. But to continue with Wharton and Codman:

It matters not if the connection between base and cornice be maintained by actual pilasters or mouldings, or by their painted or woven imitations. The line, and not the substance, is what the eye demands.

The decorator is . . . not to explain illusions, but to produce them.

The two sentences above are a great statement of a classical principle. Classical architecture lies to tell a great truth.

We are edging into the purlieus of ethics in architecture, a
matter dealt with by Geoffrey Scott in Chapter V of *The Architecture of Humanism.* Let us have Wharton and Codman on the subject:

> To some minds the concealed door represents one of those ar-
> chitectural deceptions which no necessity can excuse.

> To those who regard its use an offense against artistic integrity,
> it must once more be pointed out that architecture addresses itself
> not to the moral sense, but to the eye. The existing confusion on
> this point is partly due to the strange analogy drawn by modern
> critics between artistic sincerity and moral law. Analogies are the
> most dangerous form of reasoning: they connect resemblances,
> but disguise facts . . .

> . . . the main lines of a room shall not be unnecessarily interrupted;
> and in certain cases it would be bad taste to disturb the equilib-
> rium of wall-spaces and decoration by introducing a visible door
> leading to some unimportant closet or passageway, of which the
> existence need not be known to any but the inmates of the house.

The "strange analogy" in which qualities that would be desirable
in humans (honesty, cleanliness, boldness, frankness, etc.) are applied to architecture is held today by 95 percent of the membership
of the American Institute of Architects and the American Institute
of Decorators, and by all graduates of "Schools of Design."

Now for a few sample counsels by Wharton and Codman on
various practical matters:

Doors

. . . a double door *(à deux battants)* is always preferable . . . [because it] . . . cannot encroach to any serious extent on the floor-space of the room.

According to the best authorities, the height of a well-proportioned doorway should be twice its width . . .

. . . in France it would not be easy to find an unpainted door . . .

Doors should always swing *into* a room.

Windows

Where there is a fine prospect, windows made of a single plate of glass are often preferred; but it must be remembered that the subdivisions of a sash, while obstructing the view, serve to establish a relation between the inside of the house and the landscape, making the latter what, *as seen from a room,* it logically ought to be: a part of the wall-decoration, in the sense of being subordinated to the same general lines.

It is sometimes said that the architects of the eighteenth century would have used large plates of glass in their windows had they been able to obtain them; but as such plates were frequently used for mirrors, it is evident that they were not difficult to get . . .

The better the house, the less need there was for curtains.

. . . the beauty of a room depending chiefly on its openings, to conceal these under draperies is to hide the key of the whole decorative scheme.

The solid inside shutter . . . formerly served the purposes for which curtains and shades are used . . .

Fireplaces

Where the mantel-piece is of wood, the setting back of the architrave [lintel of a mantelpiece] is a necessity; but curiously enough, the practice has become so common in England and America that even where the mantel is made of marble or stone it is set back in the same way . . .

The early American fireplace was merely a cheap provincial copy of English models of the same period. The application of the word "Colonial" to pre-Revolutionary architecture and decoration has created a vague impression that there existed at that time an American architectural style. As a matter of fact, "Colonial" architecture is simply a modest copy of Georgian models . . .

Andirons should be of wrought-iron, bronze or ormolu. Substances which require constant polishing, such as steel or brass, are unfitted to a fireplace.

Interior cornices

A coved ceiling greatly increases the apparent height of a low-studded room; but rooms of this kind should not be treated with an order, since the projection of the cornice below the springing of the cove will lower the walls so much as to defeat the purpose for which the cove has been used.

Durand, in his lectures on architecture, in speaking of cornices lays down the following excellent rules: "Interior cornices must necessarily differ more or less from those belonging to the orders as used externally, though in rooms of reasonable height these differences need be but slight; but if the stud be low, as sometimes is inevitable, the cornice must be correspondingly narrowed, and given an excessive projection, in order to increase the apparent height of the room. Moreover, as in the interior of the house the light is much less bright than outside, the cornice should be so profiled that the juncture of the mouldings shall form not right angles, but acute angles, with spaces between the mouldings serving to detach the latter still more clearly from each other." [This was done in "A Georgian Panelled Room," *Classical America* IV. It was copied from a Mansart drawing, but until I read this I never knew why it was done.]

From diverse architectural elements, let us turn to rooms, and observe *suitability* in practice:

The Main Hall and Staircase

. . . it is difficult to see whence the modern architect has derived his idea of the combined hall and staircase.

. . . there is no good reason for uniting them and there are many for keeping them apart.

The staircase in a private house is for the use of those who inhabit it; the vestibule or hall is necessarily used by persons in no way concerned with the private life of the inmates.

The furniture of the hall should consist of benches or straight-backed chairs, and marble-topped tables and consoles. If a press is used, it should be architectural in design, like the old French and Italian *armoires* painted with arabesques and architectural motives, or the English seventeenth-century presses made of some warm-toned wood like walnut and surmounted by a broken pediment with a vase or bust in the centre.

For the lighting of the hall there should be a lantern like that in the vestibule, but more elaborate in design. This mode of light-

METAL STAIRWAY BANNISTER IN THE SAN
FRANCISCO CITY HALL

(DESIGNED BY ARTHUR BROWN, JR.)

Henry Hope Reed

ing harmonizes with the severe treatment of the walls and indicates at once that the hall is not a livingroom, but a thoroughfare.

Where the walls of a hall are hung with pictures, these should
be few in number, and decorative in composition and coloring.

I can remember when the halls of the great New York apartment houses were like the description above, with console tables
with wrought iron bases, urns on columns, lanterns, and walls of
stone or marble. Today these lobbies have sofas with coffee-tables,
end-tables with drum lampshades, and very likely a luminous ceiling hung below the original coffered vaulting. *When* suitability
departs, every room tends to become a living room. All the houses of
Horace Trumbauer—the Duke House at the corner of Fifth Avenue and Seventy-eighth Street (now the Institute of Fine Arts of
New York University) may be familiar—conform to the Wharton-
Codman precepts, which are after all traditional and not something the authors made up. They are not original.

In passing, the originality prized so much by advocates of modern art and architecture—*vide The Architecture of Humanism,* Chapter VI—is not valued much by those of the classical persuasion. All
great architects from the Renaissance to the present have believed
they were following a style of the past.

Originality in the sense that we find it acceptable and desirable
is the transfer of remembered forms to new contexts. Gabriel,
when he built the Place de la Concorde, said: "I am working in the
style of the Great Century" (meaning the time of Louis XIV). He
meant that he was inspired by the Perrault front of the Louvre.
Bramante, when he considered the rebuilding of St. Peter's, said:
"We must put the Pantheon on top of the Basilica of Maxentius."
The backward glance transforms. The copies look nothing like the
prototypes.

But to return to the authors of *The Decoration of Houses*, they make a most telling point in their discussion of the true purposes of great rooms in a classical house, or in proper translation, *le salon de compagnie:*

> In the grandest houses of Europe the gala-rooms are never thrown open except for general entertainments . . . the spectacle of a dozen people languishing after dinner in the gilded wilderness of a state saloon is practically unknown.
>
> . . . half of the chairs should be so light . . . that groups may be formed and broken up at will. The walls should be brilliantly decorated, without needless elaboration of detail . . .
>
> The lighting of the company drawing-room . . . should be evenly diffused, without the separate centres of illumination needful in a family living-room.

If this advice would only be taken, how much better life would be. Take a large house at Princeton after the Navy game. The poor old family living rooms are pressed into service for the descending mob who find themselves thrust into deep chairs they can't get out of when they are introduced. When they stand up they are dazzled by looking down into lampshades, they bark their shins on coffee tables, and they are exhausted from standing up because there aren't enough chairs, since the space is filled with big comfies with guys and gals perched on the arms. Nobody ever has a very good time at these "kermesses" because of the *unsuitability* of the rooms.

As Wharton and Codman take care to point out, our architects when called upon to build a grand house have simply enlarged rather than altered the maison bourgeoise (e.g., the Vanderbilt house at Hyde Park). In a house which is an enlargement of an ordinary dwelling, the hostess is compelled to use the *salon de compagnie* as a drawing room. Occupied by small numbers of people, such a room ("a gilded wilderness") looks out of proportion, stiff and empty. The hostess then sets chairs and tables askew, and introduces screens and knick-knacks to produce informality. The room dwarfs the furniture, loses its air of state, and gains little in comfort. When a party is given it becomes necessary to remove the furniture and disarrange the house; thus undoing the chief *raison d'être* of such apartments. The point is crisply made in the *Decoration of Houses:*

> This confusion of two essentially different types of room, designed for essentially different phases of life, has been caused by the fact that the architect, when called upon to build a grand house, has simply enlarged, instead of altering, the *maison bourgeoise* that has hitherto been the accepted model of the American gentleman's house . . .

> A gala room is never meant to be seen except when crowded: the crowd takes the place of furniture.

> Gala rooms are meant for general entertainments, never for any assemblage small or informal enough to be conveniently accommodated in the ordinary living-rooms of the house; therefore to fulfil their purpose they must be large, very high-studded, and not overcrowded with furniture . . .

A good example of a gala room in a current restoration is the octagonal room at the Morris-Jumel house (1765) in Manhattan. The room has been *suitably* furnished by Mrs. Justin Haynes, the well-known authority.

Here are Wharton and Codman on the subject of great gala room decoration in Italy:

> Sometimes the "grand manner"—the mimic *terribilità*—may be carried too far to suit Anglo-Saxon taste—it is hard to say for what form of entertainment such a room as Giulio Romano's Sala dei

Giganti in the Palazzo del Te would form a pleasing or appropriate background—but apart from such occasional aberrations, the
Italian decorators showed a wonderful sense of fitness in the treatment of state apartments. To small dribbles of ornament they
preferred bold forcible mouldings, coarse but clear-cut free-hand
ornamentation in stucco, and either a classic severity of treatment
or the turbulent bravura style of the saloon of the Villa Rotonda
and of Tiepolo's Cleopatra frescoes in the Palazzo Labia at Venice.

The Italian decorator held any audacity permissible in a room
used only by a throng of people, whose mood and dress made
them ready to accept the fairy-tales on the walls as a fitting background to their own masquerading.

. . . such apartments were meant to be seen by the soft light of wax
candles in crystal chandeliers, with fantastically dressed dancers
thronging the marble floor.

Such a ball-room, if reproduced in the present day, would be
far more effective than the conventional white-and-gold room,
which, though unobjectionable when well decorated, lacks the
imaginative charm, the personal note, given by the painter's
touch.

A panelling of mirrors forms a brilliant ball-room decoration
[The old Hewitt house on Lexington Avenue had a mirrored
dado], and charming effects are produced by painting these mirrors with birds, butterflies, and garlands of flowers . . .

All this may sound out of place in today's houses, but think of
the vast new fortunes which have yet to be bitten by the building
bug, the *manie de bâtir*. How could they be with the Modern
Movement in fashion? Clubs, embassies, conference centers, ho-

tels, governor's mansions, and houses await the Apollonian touch of the classical architect-decorator.

How much influence did this book actually have? I would say that it killed off once and for all rooms in different styles in the same house: no more Gothic smoking rooms. It leveled a fatal shaft at the big houses of the best firms when it said that they were *maisons bourgeoises* enlarged. The houses of Horace Trumbauer, Charles Platt, David Adler, Mott B. Schmidt, Delano and Aldrich, Victor Proetz and Bancel LaFarge—our best houses, in short—are complete exemplars of all that this book sets forth. *The Decoration of Houses* was certainly studied by Elsie de Wolfe and her circle, and by William Odom, who founded the Parsons School of Design. This school in its heyday was completely in the Wharton and Codman vein, and trained many decorators. Mrs. Archibald Manning Brown of McMillen, Inc., was perhaps the foremost exponent along with Alavoine et Cie. of the French house in that brief time between World War I and the Depression, and in a smaller way into the forties. Wharton and Codman expanded our architectural horizons and our social horizons as well, by showing us a finer, more developed style of living, the style of *la France civilisatrice.*

In one way, Wharton and Codman were, alas, wrong. They believed that their ideas would be adopted *chez les meilleurs,* and that those below them in the pecking order would emulate those above, and thus their wisdom would be spread. This was the norm in a class society, but the social pyramid—once so glossy and steep —has disappeared and we have instead a cluster of ethnic towers à la San Gimignano.

With the Depression came Modern Art. "Thy hand great Anarch! let the curtain fall and universal darkness buries all," in

Alexander Pope's resonant phrases. Architects and decorators were told to make themselves anew rather than extend the long chain of the classical tradition. Everything that could not be defended by rational argument was thrown out. To strip art of its sheath (the fennel of Prometheus*) of transcendence—that element which is at the heart of all religions—has been a continuing modern motif, but when transcendence is cast out, everything that makes art is cast out too. The rationalist's reason is like King Midas's fulfilled wish. Everything it touches dies. Classical art died . . . but only for a time.

*Prometheus brought fire from the chariot of the sun in a stalk of fennel.

THE GENESIS OF A CLASSIC
BY WILLIAM A. COLES

It may seem perverse to start a book concentrating on 18th century English decoration in New York in the 1890s, but a good case can be made for arguing that interior decoration as we know it to-day started with Edith Wharton, who in collaboration with Ogden Codman wrote *The Decoration of Houses.*

So opens *English Decoration in the Eighteenth Century* by John Fowler and John Cornforth, one of the most knowledgeable books on interior decoration to appear in recent decades. Whether or not one accepts the authors' contention, there is no disputing the influence of the Wharton-Codman book, nor the weight and seriousness of its approach to the subject. *The Decoration of Houses* is a *classical* text in the fullest sense of the word.

That a book of such authority should have been written by Edith Wharton and Ogden Codman in 1897 would not then have been expected. For Mrs. Wharton's international reputation as a novelist, a woman of exacting standards of taste, and a perfection-ist hostess to an exceptionally discriminating circle of friends lay entirely in the future. Nor did Codman's skills as an architect and interior decorator, though already in evidence, either then or afterwards ever bring him great reknown, as John Fowler and John Cornforth's just-quoted remark would suggest. To the English writers he is no more than a dependent clause to Mrs. Wharton's endeavor.

The history of the composition of this triumphantly impersonal and authoritative book is, perhaps fittingly, elusive. Later in his life Ogden Codman is reported to have claimed that *he* wrote the book and Mrs. Wharton merely polished the style. The story would seem to smack of a desire, in part understandable, to retaliate against Mrs. Wharton's reputation, which had eclipsed his own role in the undertaking. Mrs. Wharton, however, far from being a ghost writer, later confessed that she herself could not write clear, concise English when she started to collaborate on the book. In her autobiography she credits her lifelong friend Walter Berry, who was staying with the Whartons after the first draft of the book was written, with helping her to revise the manuscript and, indeed, with teaching her how to write effectively. Moreover, Daniel Berkeley Updike, the man responsible for the appropriately classical design of the book when it appeared in print, who had been introduced to Mrs. Wharton at Newport by Codman and would presumably have known about the collaboration, never questions it in his account of the book. I see no reason to doubt that *The Decoration of Houses* was the result of a genuine meeting of minds and sharing of ideas between Edith Wharton and Ogden Codman, both of whom, as we shall see, by the time the book was written, had acquired the knowledge and concrete experience necessary to write it.

Apart from the authorship, the account of circumstances lead-

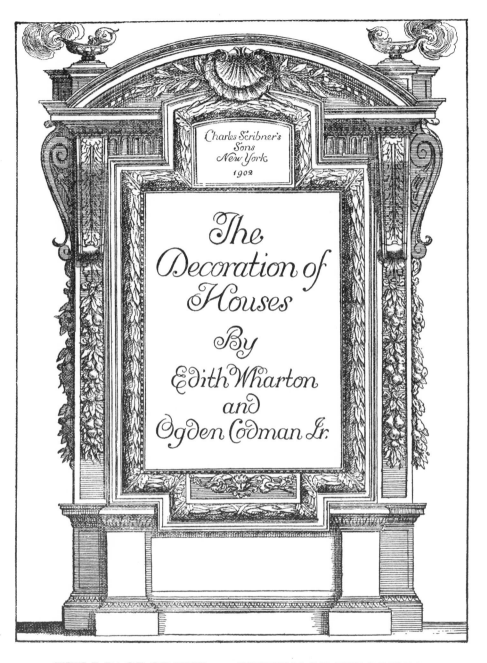

Charles Scribner's
Sons
New York
1902

The
Decoration of
Houses
By
Edith Wharton
and
Ogden Codman Jr.

TITLE PAGE OF THE 1902 EDITION OF *THE DECORA-*
TION OF HOUSES.

ing up to the venture has become confused, in large measure owing to Mrs. Wharton's faulty recollection of the event in later years. However, it is now possible to clarify the story. In her account of the book in *A Backward Glance*, Mrs. Wharton silently telescopes the events of almost a decade into one year. She seems to imply that alterations and decorations at "Land's End," the Wharton's house in Newport, which were entrusted to Ogden Codman, "a clever young Boston architect," led in direct sequence to collaboration on a book expressing their shared values in interior decoration. Moreover, she also implies that this sequence took place only one year after she had begun to write poetry again as an adult and had submitted her work, for the first time, with success to *Scribner's Magazine*. One of the poems she mentions in her account is "The Last Giustiniani," whose acceptance lingered in her memory as the virtual inauguration of her literary career.

In fact she had written "The Last Giustiniani" back in 1889. In that year Mrs. Wharton, having inherited a substantial legacy, which, together with a legacy from her father, gave her a very comfortable income, took her first independent house in New York, on Madison Avenue. It was here that her first letter of acceptance arrived. In 1891 she followed up this venture by purchasing a tiny house at 884 Park Avenue; a few years later she added the house next door at 882. During this period she had also begun to write prose. A sketch was accepted and published in *Scribner's* in 1890; in 1891 she wrote a short story and the following year she worked on a novella which was not to appear in print for many years. It was only in 1893 that Mrs. Wharton bought "Land's End," a substantial property at Newport, across the island from her mother's house, "Pencraig," and from the smaller "Pencraig

Cottage" across the road, in which the Whartons had lived during the first years of their marriage.[1] The Whartons then began to work with Ogden Codman on the interior remodeling of their new house. The year 1893, however, stands out as a landmark year in American architecture and the fact that it coincided with Mrs. Wharton's private architectural preoccupations is a curious but nonetheless significant fact.

Eighteen ninety-three was the year of the World's Columbian Exposition in Chicago, notable, above all, for its splendid Court of Honor in which monumental classical planning, architectural composition, and decorative painting and sculpture were introduced to America on a vast and heroic scale. Newspapers and magazines were full of stories about the fair and the artistic Renaissance which it heralded\ for America. The concept of a great concert of the arts, collaborating under the guidance of architecture to submerge idiosyncracy in the realization of a noble ideal was a central theme of the enterprise. It was later stressed by Henry Adams in his response to the fair, recounted in his autobiography, and also by the French novelist, Paul Bourget, who came to America, among other things, to see and report on the fair. In the early autumn of 1893 Bourget was one of the first guests to be entertained at "Land's End."

Mrs. Wharton's own career had evolved slowly but surely towards an interest in the decorative arts. She had spent a large portion of her youth in Europe, whose artistic splendors rendered especially painful her return to the brownstone comforts of her native city. In 1885, the year of her marriage, Egerton Winthrop,

[1]Berkeley Updike is surely remembering incorrectly when he implies that Mrs. Wharton was still living in "Pencraig Cottage" in 1897, when her literary collaboration with Codman took place.

a cultivated American expatriate, by a fortunate coincidence had returned to New York and became a close friend of the Whartons. Winthrop was a discerning connoisseur and together with Julian Story, the son of the sculptor William Wetmore Story, he fostered Mrs. Wharton's developing interest in the decorative arts and particularly the arts of *settecento* Italy. The Whartons and Winthrop began to travel annually, exploring both the highways and byways of the Italian peninsula. It was during this period that Mrs. Wharton's friendship with Ogden Codman began. However, it was specifically through Paul Bourget that her interests and pastimes took a more serious turn. In 1894 Bourget introduced her to Violet Paget ("Vernon Lee"), the Anglo-Florentine aesthete, whose knowledge of Italian art, architecture, and gardening was very extensive. She too was a devotee of, and guide to, the Italian *settecento*. She was also one of the most brilliant women of her day. Under the influence of such cultivated and discerning amateurs (the day of the professional scholar in such matters, we may remember, had scarcely dawned), Mrs. Wharton's taste, experience, and convictions quickly deepened. She even wrote her first sketch on an art subject at this time, an account of the little-known sculptures of the Way of the Cross at San Vivaldo, later to be included in her volume *Italian Backgrounds*. Meanwhile she continued to write some poems and stories. Two more stories were accepted by Scribner's in 1893 and the firm even suggested the possibility of publishing a volume of her sketches and stories.

However, at this point there is a pause in Mrs. Wharton's development. From late 1894 till the end of 1896 she was experiencing and recuperating from a nervous collapse which obviously weakened her self-confidence. This was a period of crisis in which dissatisfactions and lack of fulfillment in her social and marital life were given sharper focus by the possibility of a more satisfying alternative way of life glimpsed in her writing and in the stimulation of her new-found friends. When she eventually recovered from this siege, she had crossed a boundary line in her development and in a sense she really never looked back thereafter. While she was recuperating from her illness Mrs. Wharton sent her editor at Scribner's two uncertain prose works, which were refused, and then three sonnets, which were accepted. But by this time Mrs. Wharton's health and self-confidence had returned and she was already at work with Codman on *The Decoration of Houses*, which brought to a happy resolution her experiences of the last decade in travel, studying and buying furniture, and interior decoration. In a sense, then, her first sustained venture as a writer was more directly distilled out of her immediate recent experience than were her first attempts at fiction.

The Decoration of Houses seems to have been written in a remarkably short time. No doubt the authors had discussed the ideas incorporated in the book during the previous years of their acquaintance. The actual writing apparently began in the winter of 1897 and an incomplete manuscript with some photos was brought to Scribner's early in the summer. It is difficult to imagine that there was time enough for the book to have been previously presented to Macmillan's and rejected, as Mrs. Wharton recounts in *A Backward Glance*. Furthermore, her relationship with Scribner's was by then, as we have seen, more substantial than she there indicates, so that one wonders why she would not have sent them the book first. In any event Scribner's accepted the manuscript, though with some reservations about its potential public. Rewriting took place under Walter Berry's tutelage in late July and August, in order to meet the publisher's deadline of September 1, and the printed book appeared promptly on December 3, 1897. From it Mrs. Wharton received the first royalty check of her life, and dividends continued for many years thereafter.

About Ogden Codman's role in the work less need be said, because interior decoration was obviously his principal talent. He had been brought up almost entirely in France and French classical architecture was his lifelong passion and field of study. His formal training, however, was not substantial. In 1882 he returned to Boston to spend an unhappy year in the newly opened MIT School of Architecture. (He later asked to have his name removed from the roles of the school.) This was followed by two "dreary" years in an architect's office in Lowell, Mass., and further apprenticeship in the Boston firm of Andrews, Jacques, and Rantoul. In his spare time, he explored Colonial architecture in and around Boston, making measured drawings of the better work, notably that of Samuel McIntyre. Along with Charles Follen McKim and Stanford White, he was among the first to study the architecture of the colonies and the early republic. His first commissions were in Newport, where he spent summers and had family connections. By 1893, the year in which he worked on Mrs. Wharton's "Land's End," he had opened an office in New York. His primary social and professional axis of Boston, Newport, and New York overlapped the Whartons' and, indeed, Mrs. Wharton lists him as one of the newer breed of men, along with Charles McKim and Stanford White, who were stirring the stale cultural air of New York. Though Codman designed nearly two dozen houses during his abbreviated career as an architect, he did much more successful work as a decorator. His houses, nevertheless, are always accomplished and correct, and sometimes quite distinguished. Before embarking on the literary project with Mrs. Wharton, he had greatly enhanced his reputation in 1895 by decorating ten bed-rooms at "The Breakers," Cornelius Vanderbilt's vast Newport *palazzo*. Subsequently his most substantial commission, apart from his own houses, the Château de Grégy and the villa "La Léopolda" in France, was the furnishing of "Kyhuit," the John D. Rockefel-ler, Jr., house in Pocantico Hills, New York.[2]

By 1897, then, both Mrs. Wharton and Ogden Codman were interested, knowledgeable, and experienced in their subject. Fur-thermore, the United States was ripe for the book they were to write and the authors themselves were well aware that they were not exactly inaugurating a new taste. Their book opens with the statement that the past ten years have been marked by a notable development in architecture and decoration, nowhere more strik-ing than in the United States. The writers are thinking of the work of such firms as McKim, Mead and White, which led the move-ment called the American Renaissance.[3] Though the Chicago Fair was the most spectacular public demonstration of the aims of these architects, the movement in which they participated had been gathering momentum for almost two decades and would continue with unabated vigor for at least three decades to come. During this period the scale of American life and artistic ambitions was trans-

[2]Codman did not design Mrs. Wharton's principal American house, "The Mount," at Lenox, Mass. (1901–1902), because, as she said, he had become too expen-sive. She turned instead to Col. Francis V. L. Hoppin, architect of the old Police Headquarters of New York City.

[3]Mrs. Wharton and Ogden Codman never directly mention Richard Morris Hunt, the father of the American Renaissance (though see below, p. 21, for discus-sion of an indirect reference by Mrs. Wharton). In the 1890s Hunt, who died two years before the publication of *The Decoration of Houses*, may have seemed more a *retardataire* figure of the Second Empire—the architect of Château-sur-Mer at New-port—to Mrs. Wharton's generation. He had, after all, practiced in the U.S. for forty years. Codman, for his part, seems to have admired little American work other than that of Horace Trumbauer.

BALLROOM AT "LA LÉOPOLDA"

(BY OGDEN CODMAN, JR.)

Society for the Preservation of New England Antiquities

MRS. WHARTON'S PARLOR AT 884 PARK AVENUE

(DECORATED BY OGDEN CODMAN, JR.)

The Metropolitan Museum of Art, Gift of the Estate of Ogden Codman, Jr.

formed. It was perhaps the most crucial period of our cultural evolution, and much that we take for granted in libraries, galleries, shops, and universities—in the sophisticated tone of our society— was either founded at this time or was given its essentially modern form.

At the beginning of this period the decoration of the Fifth Avenue mansions of William K. Vanderbilt and Cornelius Vanderbilt had a particularly strong influence on the development of interior decoration in the country. By the end of the decade of the eighties most important Paris art dealers had either representatives or branches in New York, in addition to important native dealers. Allard et Fils (later to merge with Alavoine et Cie.), the greatest French decorators, whose origins extended back into the eighteenth century, were established in the city and could provide rooms both of old paneling and of modern work in the period styles (the prestige of the former over the latter was not yet firmly accepted). Other decorators, of course, followed suit. Moreover, stone workers, workers in marble and mosaic, wrought iron, bronze, decorative plasterwork, and other architectural crafts set up in New York and other cities to provide work essential to interiors conceived in the grand tradition. The greatest of French and English mural painters, men like Paul Baudry, J. J. Benjamin-Constant, P. V. Galland, and Sir Frederick Leighton, also executed commissions for American private houses, increasingly supplemented by the contributions of an emerging native school of decorative painters. Such options as Ogden Codman and Edith Wharton offer for the treatment of walls, ceilings, and floors of formal and gala rooms—frescoes, stucco work, tapestries, paneling, and marble pavements—were neither evocations of a forgotten and lamented European past nor of a distantly glimpsed future, but were already appearing ever more frequently in the finest American public and private buildings. *The Decoration of Houses* did not initiate this taste, but rather explained it, ordered and corrected it, rationalized it, and related it to the historical tradition of decoration, thus making it more available to laymen of cultivated taste.

Furthermore, the estrangement between architecture and decoration—or between interior and exterior architecture, if you will—which had turned later nineteenth-century rooms into labyrinths of upholstery and bric-à-brac, and was the starting point of *The Decoration of Houses'* campaign, had already begun to lessen. Twenty years before Codman and Wharton wrote, the Boston architect Henry Van Brunt had published a series of articles in *The American Architect and Building News* in which he attempted to explain interior decoration from the architect's point of view and to show that it could follow rational procedures rather than sheer whim or fashion. Almost a decade later, in 1885, Mrs. Schuyler Van Rensselaer, reviewing recent architecture for the *Century Magazine,* had singled out McKim, Mead and White's Villard Houses in New York as having the best interiors in the country and showing the architect's new-found involvement in decoration. Three years later architect Bruce Price was making a case for the architect's superiority to the decorator in his feeling for harmony between rooms, proportion within rooms, and for effects achieved through wood, stone, bronze, and marble, rather than stuffs, paint, and paper. While Richard Morris Hunt, the leader of the American Renaissance, seems as an architect to have been less involved himself in interior work, he at the very least encouraged his clients to work with decorators like Allard, who thoroughly understood the architectural approach to their calling.

It is important to understand that when Codman and Wharton

maintain that house decoration must be treated as a branch of architecture they are not necessarily suggesting that the architect and the decorator must be, and always have been, the same person in the great periods of interior decoration. They are rather saying that the decorator must conceive of his function architecturally, that is, in terms of the fundamental architecture of the room, rather than the mere *adding* of ornament *to* the room. That architecture was more firmly in control of decoration during its greatest periods is beyond question, but the matter of the evolution of the interior decorator as a separate entity and the relationship of architect to upholsterer/furnisher/decorator is an intriguing and complex subject—more complex, perhaps, than Codman and Mrs. Wharton suggest. It is a curious fact that we are just beginning to inquire into and learn something about the history of the interior decorator, whose influence on modern life has been, after all, both pervasive and profound.

Hitherto most histories of decoration have been simply histories of furniture and styles and they tell us next to nothing about how the elements they discuss were ordered and assembled. In actuality, with respect to the architect's involvement in details of furnishing and the finishing of interiors, there would seem to have been no settled practice. In all likelihood, conditions varied according to the predilection of the architect and client, the significance and scope of a particular commission, or the importance and wealth of the patron. What seems likely is that as interiors themselves became more complex—that is, by the eighteenth century —when types of furniture had become very varied and specialized, when a wide variety of fabrics existed, when there were many different kinds of rooms and apartments and many different possibilities for the treatment of walls, windows, and floors, the decorator emerged, either from among the various workmen and contractors, as, for instance, the upholsterer, to coordinate work, or appeared from outside as a dealer or agent who commissioned work from various craftsmen or handled their goods. In the sixteenth century, the greater part of an interior *was* fundamentally architecture. By the mid-eighteenth century much of an interior, especially in more intimate apartments, depended on furnishings and upholsterer's work. In a sense domestic comfort became the province of the various tradesmen and brought forth the need for the overseeing decorator. By the late-nineteenth century, when classical style reasserted itself and reined in the vagaries of restless taste, it was again essential for architecture to reclaim its original control over the development of interiors and to do so in the name of reason, order, and simplicity. The Wharton-Codman book attempts to meet this need.

What is most striking about *The Decoration of Houses* is the absolute assurance and authority of its point of view. No equivocations here about personal taste or expression, but rather a resumption of the great tradition of architecture and decoration such as had been boldly made four years earlier in the Court of Honor at the Chicago Exposition. "After a period of eclecticism," say the authors, "that has lasted long enough to make architects and decorators lose their traditional habits of design, there has arisen a sudden demand for 'style.' It necessarily follows that only the most competent are ready to respond to this unexpected summons. Much has to be relearned, still more to be unlearned. The essence of the great styles lay in proportion and the science of proportion is not to be acquired in a day." In a way there is more of youth than of age in the somewhat brash way in which the authors here gather the mantle of tradition around themselves and discount an outworn taste. One is reminded of the early writings of T. S. Eliot, both in tone and in the concern manifested for the resumption of a lapsed tradition.

The authoritative note of the book is also apparent in the prefactory list of works consulted. Du Cerceau, Oppenord, d'Aviler, Blondel, Roubo, Percier et Fontaine, Quatremère de Quincy, Letarouilly, Isaac Ware, Colen Campbell, the Adam brothers, Hepplewhite, and Sheraton are among the sources listed. Nothing even remotely savors of Eastlake or the *Lady's Book*. The same rigor guided the selection of plates which originally illustrated the text. English rooms and details were taken from a Georgian town house by William Kent in Berkeley Square, "Easton Neston," and "Audley End." French illustrations came from the Grand Trianon; the palace of Versailles; the Petit Trianon; Chantilly; Fontainebleau; Compiègne; the Palais de Justice, Rennes; and the Hôtel de Ville, Nancy. Italian sources were the Villa Vertemati; the Ducal Palace, Mantua; the Palazzo del Te; the Ducal Palace, Urbino; the Villa Giacomelli; the Villa Cambiaso, Genoa; the Durazzo Palace, Genoa; the Royal Palace, Genoa; and the Pitti Palace.

The authors are aware that while much is said of simplicity in the text, the illustrations are taken from buildings of considerable importance. (Mrs. Wharton's statement in *A Backward Glance* that she and Codman "had purposely excluded palaces and royal châteaux from our list, and directed the attention of our readers to the study of small and simple houses," is surely somewhat disingenuous.) Nevertheless they attempt to justify their selection by saying that the reader will be more interested in rooms that are accessible to the traveler, and that also the most magnificent palaces contain rooms that are as simple as can be found in any private houses. The excuse is not altogether convincing, and it is easy to see that the authors intend Americans henceforth to develop their taste on the highest and best models. The scale of American aspiration in architecture has now become thoroughly cosmopolitan. Our Roman republican origins during this period matured into an imperial Roman eclecticism. Behind Wharton and Codman's work lies the hope that some at least of their readers will be inspired not merely to redecorate, but to build nobly:

> If it be granted [they say] that a reform in house decoration, if not necessary, is at least desirable, it must be admitted that such reform can originate only with those whose means permit of any experiments which their taste may suggest. When the rich man demands good architecture his neighbors will get it too. The vulgarity of current decoration has its source in the indifference of the wealthy to architectural fitness. Every good moulding, every carefully studied detail, exacted by those who can afford to indulge their taste, will in time find its way to the carpenter-built cottage. Once the right precedent has been established, it costs less to follow than to oppose it.

The reference to proportion in a passage previously quoted from the book provides the key to the authors' architectural values. Their work, as they stress, is a study of *"house decoration as a branch of architecture."* They are not offering a manual of styles and periods or hints for dressing up rooms. They are concerned to emphasize the fundamental principles that underlie the best instances of interior decoration which are most appropriate to our mode of life, and they leave it to others, like Elsie de Wolfe,[4] to add the "per-

---

[4]There is no question that Elsie de Wolfe was much influenced by the Wharton-Codman volume in writing her own book, *The House in Good Taste*, which both disseminated and diluted its predecessor's ideals. She maintained a friendship with Codman over the years, seeing him frequently in France, but I can find no indication of a connection with Mrs. Wharton, though there must have been many opportunities for the two to meet. One suspects that their values and temperaments

sonal touches" and the vulgarly cozy chattiness which so often
seem to characterize successful interior decorators and to suit their
clients' tastes.

If the authors see proportion as the "good breeding of architecture," they define symmetry, or the answering of one part to
another, as the "sanity of decoration." The two values are the basis
of all achievement. Accordingly, while praising Ruskin as a guide
to the byways of art, they call his notions of beauty into question:

> For years [they write] he has spent the full force of his unmatched
> prose in denouncing the enormity of putting a door or a window
> in a certain place in order that it may correspond to another; nor
> has he scrupled to declare to the victims of this practice that it
> leads to abysses of moral as well as artistic degradation.

> Time has taken the terror from these threats and architects are
> beginning to see that a regard for external symmetry, far from
> interfering with the requirements of house-planning, tends to
> produce a better, because a more carefully studied, plan, as well
> as a more convenient distribution of wall-space. . . . It is, therefore,
> not superfluous to point out that, in interior decoration as well as
> in architecture, a regard for symmetry, besides satisfying a legiti-
> mate artistic requirement, tends to make the average room not
> only easier to furnish, but more comfortable to live in.

The Decoration of Houses not only espouses classical principles,
but it incorporates them into its own style and structure. The book
is designed with the perfect symmetry of a French classical drama.
An opening chapter presents the subject in its historical perspective, allowing us to see how taste in decoration has evolved. The
last chapter discusses a specific problem of the historical moment

---

were not likely to accord and a simple comparison of the titles of their two books
would serve to indicate why.

at which the book appeared, the taste for bric-à-brac which has obscured the difference between fine workmanship and vulgar ornamentation, and has cluttered interiors. In between, the first half of the book deals with the fundamental structural components of a room, walls, doors, windows, fireplaces, ceilings, and floors; the second half deals with the main types of rooms, categorized according to usage, from the entrance and vestibule of the house to the bedrooms and nurseries. The organization, then, is architectural, and in contrast to such books as Eastlake's *Hints on Household Taste*, furniture plays a distinctly subordinate role in the work.

The architect's task is to achieve a proper placement and proportion of opening to wall. It is important to bear in mind the relation of furniture to ornament and of each room as a whole to others in the house. There should be no violent break in the continuity of treatment from room to room: "Every house should be decorated according to a carefully graduated scale of ornamentation culminating in the most important room of the house." Though not always possible, it is best when decoration and furniture are chosen together. Each ought to be chosen with reference to the other. Therefore the decorator should know what furniture a room is to contain before he plans his treatment.

Aesthetic priorities in the book are thoroughly consistent with abundant concern for comfort and a thorough absence of snobbery and pretentiousness. There is ample treatment of the epic opportunities for decoration, unlike today when the concept and role of splendor cause embarrassment and fortunes can be tossed away on ill-conceived and inappropriate effects. Indeed, one of the notable aspects of the book is that it confronts and addresses itself to the possibilities of such work in America; but there is no disposition to allow epic ambition to outstrip capacities. It is only in rooms dedicated to entertainment, say the authors, where little furniture is used, that more elaborate schemes of decoration may be properly used. But where a room is to be decorated at the smallest possible cost, there is wholesome advice about reserving the most money available for comfortable chairs and sofas and substantial tables, while merely tinting the walls a uniform color and putting the simplest carpet on the floor. All cheap devices of disguise are properly eschewed. "There are but two ways of dealing with a room that is fundamentally ugly," they conclude; "one is to accept it, and the other is courageously to correct its ugliness. Half-way remedies are a waste of money and serve rather to call attention to the defects of the room than to conceal them."

As an instance of the authors' general method, the chapter on walls will serve. The fundamental premise is laid out that the wall is in reality an order, generally simplified and to some extent abstracted, but with the essential proportional rhythm of base, shaft, and capital, transferred to dado, intervening space, and cornice. Any decorative scheme must adjust the proportions of all elements and relate to the furniture to be placed against the walls. Under wall decorations the authors examine first the noblest forms, fresco painting, paneling, and tapestry hangings, taking care to correct the historical and psychological errors of writers like Ruskin with respect to the propriety of using stucco paneling or woven, that is, tapestry, mouldings. The decorative artist is justified in presenting to the eye whatever his skill can devise to satisfy its requirements. There is no such thing as deception to the artist; only suitability and effectiveness.

The authors then explain the development under differing conditions of paneling in stone, marble, stucco, or wood, and they examine their various decorative possibilities. Under fresco they

AN ELEVATION OF AN INTERIOR OF "THE
BREAKERS" AS RENDERED BY CODMAN

remind their readers that the large heroic style of painting was only one of its phases, and that more intimate schemes, such as Pompeian-style arabesques were also used. And they correctly point out that the demand for a kind of decoration would call forth talent to produce it. Many artists who waste their energies on indifferent easel work might more usefully employ their talents on decorative painting, properly understood.

Next the use of wallpapers or immovable fabric panels are objected to on grounds both of appearance and cleanliness (conditions today might mitigate these objections), and a final glance is given to the wall as a proper background for pictures. Though a full scale of the decorative treatment of walls has been touched upon, the authors conclude by noting that "where the walls are treated in an architectural manner, with a well-designed dado and cornice, and an over-mantel and overdoors connecting the openings with the cornice, it will be found that in a room of average size the intervening wall spaces may be tinted in a uniform color and left unornamented." When the fundamental lines are right, little need be done to complete the effect; when they are wrong, no overlaying of ornament will conceal the deficiencies. The more common level of experience, then, is seen from the point of view of the same *general* values which underlie the richest examples.

The second half of *The Decoration of Houses* is given over to an examination of the house in terms of the nature, purpose, and proper treatment of each room. Once again, the possibility of the use of elaborate and formal rooms, such as a ballroom or music room, is assumed, but the treatment given to the entire panorama of types also serves the purpose of distinguishing between overlapping instances and *confused* types. In general the authors believe that a room should have a distinct function and that the tendency to combine functions is more likely to multiply dissatisfaction than to satisfy several needs at once. In their several chapters they attempt to follow the evolution of the *use* of each room. In distinguishing, for instance, between the *salon de compagnie* and the *salon de famille*, they can thereby destroy the "best parlor" superstition, which results from imposing the idea of the former upon circumstances which admit only the latter. They note the curious amount of money and thought frequently spent in America on the one room in the house used by no one, or occupied at most for an hour after a "company" dinner. "The *salon de compagnie*," they write, "is out of place in the average house. Such a room is needed only where the dinners or other entertainments given are so large as to make it impossible to use the ordinary living rooms of the house. In the grandest houses of Europe, the gala-rooms are never thrown open except for general entertainments or to receive guests of exalted rank, and the spectacle of a dozen people languishing after dinner in the gilded wilderness of a state saloon is practically unknown." Nevertheless, when the authors come to treat the *salon de compagnie* they give it its proper attention and explain the need for brilliant decoration requiring little close inspection, easily moved seating, and a few bold accents in furniture, statues, and vases. Nothing weak can be admitted.

The authors' use of history to explain the evolution of the *idea* of a room reveals a pervasive influence on their thought, which distinguishes them from any writers before the nineteenth century. The influence is perhaps most immediately derived from the writings of the encyclopedic Frenchman, Eugène-Emmanuel Viollet-le-Duc, who taught the age to see that styles and forms were not mere matters of taste, but were related to practical needs, uses, and modes of life, as well as to the aims and values of society. He taught, in other words, more fully and coherently than any other writer of the century, the relationship between art and life. But in acquiring historical insight Wharton and Codman use history not to minister helplessly to relativism by asserting that, after all, every age has its peculiar aims and values and all are equally useful and significant. Rather, they point out that conditions of domestic life are not endlessly in flux, but that, once the *proper* conditions had been established for settled domestic comfort, patterns gradually evolved to realize that comfort most properly and attractively. They aim to perceive the real significance of tradition and they understand that it is *change* which must justify its appropriateness. It is also refreshing to find that while the authors give a great deal of attention to the conditions of life in America, they do not accept those conditions with passive inevitability as peculiar to our unique society. They never talk about the need to express the American character or evolve a national style, because they presumably understand that such matters are never the *conscious* concerns of any artist. For them a proper decorative ideal takes precedence over national habits when those habits are slovenly. They would never consider such practices the unconscious evolution of a new pattern of life. One of the choicest passages of the book, the beginning of the chapter on doors, will serve to illustrate the point: "The fate of the door in America has been a curious one, and had the other chief features of the house—such as windows, fireplaces, and stairs—been pursued with the same relentless animosity by architects and decorators, we should no longer be living in houses at all." So much for the "space flow" of the shingle style and later the ranch house. However, behind the passage also lies an implicit aesthetic philosophy of life, which resists blurring of usage, manners, and values; which prizes privacy, order, and decorum.

The concern shown in *The Decoration of Houses* for the relationship between art and life is also manifested in Mrs. Wharton's later books, especially those on art and travel. She is always looking for larger organic relationships, whether they be between house and garden; between garden and region, climate, and way of life; between house, street, and city; or between city and national values. This feeling for the organic ties of life underlies the chapter on the decoration of the nursery and schoolroom, for which Mrs. Wharton and Codman have latterly been laughed at by the generation of Dr. Spock and Donald Duck. If, the authors feel, good design and art are important, they ought to be part of the very texture of life, imbibed in childhood and constantly nourishing the evolution of our values and our way of living. The authors deserve praise, not scorn, for a concern not shared by most other writers on decoration. One can feel Mrs. Wharton, at least, here bringing her own experience as a child to bear on the subject.

This organic sensibility also helps to explain a significant passage in Mrs. Wharton's novel, *The Custom of the Country*, in which Ralph Marvell, a representative of old New York, muses on the relationship between the "fast" new society of the city and the houses it builds:

> . . . What Popple called society was really just like the houses it lived in: a muddle of misapplied ornament over a thin steel shell of utility. The steel shell was built up in Wall Street, the social trimmings were hastily added on Fifth Avenue; and union between them was as monstrous and factitious, as unlike the gradual homogeneous growth which flowers into what other countries know as society, as that between the Blois gargoyles on Peter van Deegan's roof and the skeleton walls supporting them.[5]

One must be especially tactful in interpreting what is surely a reference here to Richard Morris Hunt's Fifth Avenue house for

[5]The Scribner Library Edition, (N.Y., n. d.), p. 73.

W. K. Vanderbilt. For one thing, the passage is the dramatic utterance, not of the narrator, but of a character whose own values, however sensitive, are seen to be flawed and insufficient to sustain life. But the passage also reflects Wharton and Codman's feeling that French Renaissance architecture, like English Tudor and Elizabethan, were relatively unsuitable to modern needs because they evolved before domestic life had reached its fully settled form of modern comfort and convenience. Even more, however, the passage in large measure incorporates Mrs. Wharton's complex feeling that our art and architecture should not merely consist of acquisitions and possessions, but be a reflection of the quality of our life and aspirations—what we ask of ourselves and are willing to live by and live up to.

In *A Backward Glance*, thinking back over the hospitality of her own parents' house, she says, "I have lingered over these details because they formed a part—a most important and honourable part—of that ancient curriculum of house-keeping which, at least in Anglo-Saxon countries, was so soon to be swept aside by the 'monstrous regiment' of the emancipated: young women taught by their elders to despise the kitchen and the linen room, and to substitute the acquiring of University degrees for the more complex art of civilized living."

For an age which has forgotten how to build with grace and nobility, the Wharton-Codman book might still usefully serve as a perfect historical guide to great houses of the past, their design, arrangements, and functions. But the book has a yet deeper and finer message for our spiritual and domestic aridities. It is really about that "more complex art of civilized living" of which Mrs. Wharton has spoken. *The Decoration of Houses* could just as appropriately be entitled *The Graces of Life,* for its real subject is not just houses but the quality of life in them, the classical question of *how to live*. Oddly enough this great book is in no way more thoroughly American than in its peculiar blend of common sense and reasoned practicality with the partly Utopian idealism that has always been necessary to lead our nation onward. It is for this quality as much as for its technical expertise, that the book remains an indispensable text.

The Decoration of Houses

By

Edith Wharton
and
Ogden Codman Jr.

*"Une forme doit être belle en elle-même et on
ne doit jamais compter sur le décor appliqué pour
en sauver les imperfections."*
HENRI MAYEUX : *La Composition Décorative.*

TABLE OF CONTENTS

LIST OF PLATES

List of Plates

List of Plates

BOOKS CONSULTED

FRENCH

ANDROUET DU CERCEAU, JACQUES.
Les Plus Excellents Bâtiments de France. *Paris, 1607.*

LE MUET, PIERRE.
Manière de Bien Bâtir pour toutes sortes de Personnes.

OPPENORD, GILLES MARIE.
Œuvres. *1750.*

MARIETTE, PIERRE JEAN.
L'Architecture Françoise. *1727.*

BRISEUX, CHARLES ÉTIENNE.
L'Art de Bâtir les Maisons de Campagne. *Paris, 1743.*

LALONDE, FRANÇOIS RICHARD DE.
Recueil de ses Œuvres.

AVILER, C. A. D'.
Cours d'Architecture. *1760.*

BLONDEL, JACQUES FRANÇOIS.
Architecture Françoise. *Paris, 1752.*
Cours d'Architecture. *Paris, 1771–77.*
De la Distribution des Maisons de Plaisance et de la Décoration
des Édifices. *Paris, 1737.*

Books Consulted

Roubo, A. J., fils.
L'Art du Menuisier.

Héré de Corny, Emmanuel.
Recueil des Plans, Élévations et Coupes des Châteaux, Jardins et Dépendances que le Roi de Pologne occupe en Lorraine. *Paris, n. d.*

Percier et Fontaine.
Choix des plus Célèbres Maisons de Plaisance de Rome et de ses Environs. *Paris, 1809.*
Palais, Maisons, et autres Édifices Modernes dessinés à Rome. *Paris, 1798.*
Résidences des Souverains. *Paris, 1833.*

Krafft et Ransonnette.
Plans, Coupes, et Élévations des plus belles Maisons et Hôtels construits à Paris et dans les Environs. *Paris, 1801.*

Durand, Jean Nicolas Louis.
Recueil et Parallèle des Édifices de tout Genre. *Paris, 1800.*
Précis des Leçons d'Architecture données à l'École Royale Polytechnique. *Paris, 1823.*

Quatremère de Quincy, A. C.
Histoire de la Vie et des Ouvrages des plus Célèbres Architectes du XIe siècle jusqu'à la fin du XVIII siècle. *Paris, 1830.*

Pellassy de l'Ousle.
Histoire du Palais de Compiègne. *Paris, n. d.*

Letarouilly, Paul Marie.
Édifices de Rome Moderne. *Paris, 1825–57.*

Books Consulted

Ramée, Daniel.
> Histoire Générale de l'Architecture. *Paris, 1862.*
> Meubles Religieux et Civils Conservés dans les principaux Monuments et Musées de l'Europe.

Viollet le Duc, Eugène Emmanuel.
> Dictionnaire Raisonné de l'Architecture Française du XIe au XVIe siècle. *Paris, 1868.*

Sauvageot, Claude.
> Palais, Châteaux, Hôtels et Maisons de France du XVe au XVIIIe siècle.

Daly, César.
> Motifs Historiques d'Architecture et de Sculpture d'Ornement.

Rouyer et Darcel.
> L'Art Architectural en France depuis François Ier jusqu'à Louis XIV.

Havard, Henry.
> Dictionnaire de l'Ameublement et de la Décoration depuis le XIIIe siècle jusqu'à nos Jours. *Paris, n. d.*
> Les Arts de l'Ameublement.

Guilmard, D.
> Les Maîtres Ornemanistes. *Paris, 1880.*

Bauchal, Charles.
> Dictionnaire des Architectes Français. *Paris, 1887.*

Rouaix, Paul.
> Les Styles. *Paris, n. d.*

Bibliothèque de l'Enseignement des Beaux Arts.
> Maison Quantin, *Paris.*

Books Consulted

ENGLISH

WARE, ISAAC.

A Complete Body of Architecture. *London, 1756.*

BRETTINGHAM, MATTHEW.

Plans, Elevations and Sections of Holkham in Norfolk, the Seat of the late Earl of Leicester. *London, 1761.*

CAMPBELL, COLEN.

Vitruvius Britannicus; or, The British Architect. *London, 1771.*

ADAM, ROBERT AND JAMES.

The Works in Architecture. *London, 1773–1822.*

HEPPLEWHITE, A.

The Cabinet-Maker and Upholsterer's Guide.

SHERATON, THOMAS.

The Cabinet-Maker's Dictionary. *London, 1803.*

PAIN, WILLIAM.

The British Palladio; or The Builder's General Assistant. *London, 1797.*

SOANE, SIR JOHN.

Sketches in Architecture. *London, 1793.*

HAKEWILL, ARTHUR WILLIAM.

General Plan and External Details, with Picturesque Illustrations, of Thorpe Hall, Peterborough.

LEWIS, JAMES.

Original Designs in Architecture.

Books Consulted

PYNE, WILLIAM HENRY.

History of the Royal Residences of Windsor Castle, St. James's Palace, Carlton House, Kensington Palace, Hampton Court, Buckingham Palace, and Frogmore. *London, 1819.*

GWILT, JOSEPH.

Encyclopedia of Architecture. New edition. *Longman's, 1895.*

FERGUSSON, JAMES.

History of Architecture. *London, 1874.*
History of the Modern Styles of Architecture. Third edition, revised by Robert Kerr. *London, 1891.*

GOTCH, JOHN ALFRED.

Architecture of the Renaissance in England.

HEATON, JOHN ALDAM.

Furniture and Decoration in England in the Eighteenth Century.

ROSENGARTEN.

Handbook of Architectural Styles. *New York, 1876.*

HORNE, H. P.

The Binding of Books. *London, 1894.*

LOFTIE, W. J.

Inigo Jones and Christopher Wren. *London, 1893.*

KERR, ROBERT.

The English Gentleman's House. *London, 1865.*

STEVENSON, J. J.

House Architecture. *London, 1880.*

Books Consulted

GERMAN AND ITALIAN

BURCKHARDT, JACOB.
Architektur der Renaissance in Italien. *Stuttgart, 1891.*

REINHARDT.
Palast Architektur von Ober Italien und Toskana.

GURLITT, CORNELIUS.
Geschichte des Barockstiles in Italien. *Stuttgart, 1887.*

EBE, GUSTAV.
Die Spät-Renaissance. *Berlin, 1886.*

LA VILLA BORGHESE, FUORI DI PORTA PINCIANA, CON L'ORNAMENTI CHE SI OSSERVANO NEL DI LEI PALAZZO. *Roma, 1700.*

INTRA, G. B.
Mantova nei suoi Monumenti.

LUZIO E RENIER.
Mantova e Urbino. *Torino-Roma, 1893.*

MOLMENTI, POMPEO.
La Storia di Venezia nella Vita Privata. *Torino, 1885.*

MALAMANI, VITTORIO.
Il Settecento a Venezia. *Milano, 1895.*

LA VITA ITALIANA NEL SEICENTO. CONFERENZE TENUTE A FIRENZE NEL 1890.

INTRODUCTION

ROOMS may be decorated in two ways: by a superficial application of ornament totally independent of structure, or by means of those architectural features which are part of the organism of every house, inside as well as out.

In the middle ages, when warfare and brigandage shaped the conditions of life, and men camped in their castles much as they did in their tents, it was natural that decorations should be portable, and that the naked walls of the mediæval chamber should be hung with arras, while a *ciel*, or ceiling, of cloth stretched across the open timbers of its roof.

When life became more secure, and when the Italian conquests of the Valois had acquainted men north of the Alps with the spirit of classic tradition, proportion and the relation of voids to masses gradually came to be regarded as the chief decorative values of the interior. Portable hangings were in consequence replaced by architectural ornament: in other words, the architecture of the room became its decoration.

This architectural treatment held its own through every change of taste until the second quarter of the present century; but since then various influences have combined to sever the natural connection between the outside of the modern house and its interior. In the average house the architect's task seems virtually confined

Introduction

to the elevations and floor-plan. The designing of what are to-day regarded as insignificant details, such as mouldings, architraves, and cornices, has become a perfunctory work, hurried over and unregarded; and when this work is done, the upholsterer is called in to " decorate " and furnish the rooms.

As the result of this division of labor, house-decoration has ceased to be a branch of architecture. The upholsterer cannot be expected to have the preliminary training necessary for architectural work, and it is inevitable that in his hands form should be sacrificed to color and composition to detail. In his ignorance of the legitimate means of producing certain effects, he is driven to all manner of expedients, the result of which is a piling up of heterogeneous ornament, a multiplication of incongruous effects; and lacking, as he does, a definite first conception, his work becomes so involved that it seems impossible for him to make an end.

The confusion resulting from these unscientific methods has reflected itself in the lay mind, and house-decoration has come to be regarded as a black art by those who have seen their rooms subjected to the manipulations of the modern upholsterer. Now, in the hands of decorators who understand the fundamental principles of their art, the surest effects are produced, not at the expense of simplicity and common sense, but by observing the requirements of both. These requirements are identical with those regulating domestic architecture, the chief end in both cases being the suitable accommodation of the inmates of the house.

The fact that this end has in a measure been lost sight of is perhaps sufficient warrant for the publication of this elementary sketch. No study of *house-decoration as a branch of architecture* has for at least fifty years been published in England or America; and though France is always producing admirable monographs

Introduction

on isolated branches of this subject, there is no modern French work corresponding with such comprehensive manuals as d'Aviler's *Cours d'Architeɛ̆ure* or Isaac Ware's *Complete Body of Architeɛ̆ure.*

The attempt to remedy this deficiency in some slight degree has made it necessary to dwell at length upon the strictly architectural principles which controlled the work of the old decorators. The effects that they aimed at having been based mainly on the due adjustment of parts, it has been impossible to explain their methods without assuming their standpoint — that of *architectural proportion* — in contradistinction to the modern view of house-decoration as *superficial application of ornament.* When house-decoration was a part of architecture all its values were founded on structural modifications; consequently it may seem that ideas to be derived from a study of such methods suggest changes too radical for those who are not building, but are merely decorating. Such changes, in fact, lie rather in the direction of alteration than of adornment; but it must be remembered that the results attained will be of greater decorative value than were an equal expenditure devoted to surface-ornament. Moreover, the great decorators, if scrupulous in the observance of architectural principles, were ever governed, in the use of ornamental detail, by the σωφροσύνη, the "wise moderation," of the Greeks; and the rooms of the past were both simpler in treatment and freer from mere embellishments than those of to-day.

Besides, if it be granted for the sake of argument that a reform in house-decoration, if not necessary, is at least desirable, it must be admitted that such reform can originate only with those whose means permit of any experiments which their taste may suggest. When the rich man demands good architecture his neighbors will

Introduction

get it too. The vulgarity of current decoration has its source in the indifference of the wealthy to architectural fitness. Every good moulding, every carefully studied detail, exacted by those who can afford to indulge their taste, will in time find its way to the carpenter-built cottage. Once the right precedent is established, it costs less to follow than to oppose it.

In conclusion, it may be well to explain the seeming lack of accord between the arguments used in this book and the illustrations chosen to interpret them. While much is said of simplicity, the illustrations used are chiefly taken from houses of some importance. This has been done in order that only such apartments as are accessible to the traveller might be given as examples. Unprofessional readers will probably be more interested in studying rooms that they have seen, or at least heard of, than those in the ordinary private dwelling; and the arguments advanced are indirectly sustained by the most ornate rooms here shown, since their effect is based on such harmony of line that their superficial ornament might be removed without loss to the composition.

Moreover, as some of the illustrations prove, the most magnificent palaces of Europe contain rooms as simple as those in any private house; and to point out that simplicity is at home even in palaces is perhaps not the least service that may be rendered to the modern decorator.

I

THE HISTORICAL TRADITION

THE last ten years have been marked by a notable development in architecture and decoration, and while France will long retain her present superiority in these arts, our own advance is perhaps more significant than that of any other country. When we measure the work recently done in the United States by the accepted architectural standards of ten years ago, the change is certainly striking, especially in view of the fact that our local architects and decorators are without the countless advantages in the way of schools, museums and libraries which are at the command of their European colleagues. In Paris, for instance, it is impossible to take even a short walk without finding inspiration in those admirable buildings, public and private, religious and secular, that bear the stamp of the most refined taste the world has known since the decline of the arts in Italy; and probably all American architects will acknowledge that no amount of travel abroad and study at home can compensate for the lack of daily familiarity with such monuments.

It is therefore all the more encouraging to note the steady advance in taste and knowledge to which the most recent architecture in America bears witness. This advance is chiefly due to the fact that American architects are beginning to perceive two things that their French colleagues, among all the modern vagaries of taste, have never quite lost sight of: first that architecture and decoration, having wandered since 1800 in a labyrinth of dubious eclecticism, can be set right only by a close study of the best models; and secondly that, given the requirements of modern life, these models are chiefly to be found in buildings erected in Italy after the beginning of the sixteenth century, and in other European countries after the full assimilation of the Italian influence.

As the latter of these propositions may perhaps be questioned by those who, in admiring the earlier styles, sometimes lose sight of their relative unfitness for modern use, it must be understood at the outset that it implies no disregard for the inherent beauties of these styles. It would be difficult, assuredly, to find buildings better suited to their original purpose than some of the great feudal castles, such as Warwick in England, or Langeais in France; and as much might be said of the grim machicolated palaces of republican Florence or Siena; but our whole mode of life has so entirely changed since the days in which these buildings were erected that they no longer answer to our needs. It is only necessary to picture the lives led in those days to see how far removed from them our present social conditions are. Inside and outside the house, all told of the unsettled condition of country or town, the danger of armed attack, the clumsy means of defence, the insecurity of property, the few opportunities of social intercourse as we understand it. A man's house was in very truth his castle in the middle ages, and in France and England especially it remained so until the end of the sixteenth century.

Thus it was that many needs arose: the tall keep of masonry

I ITALIAN GOTHIC CHEST

MUSEUM OF THE BARGELLO, FLORENCE

II FRENCH CHAIRS

FROM THE GAVET COLLECTION. XV AND XVI CENTURIES

where the inmates, pent up against attack, awaited the signal of the watchman who, from his platform or *échauguette*, gave warning of assault; the ponderous doors, oak-ribbed and metal-studded, with doorways often narrowed to prevent entrance of two abreast, and so low that the incomer had to bend his head; the windows that were mere openings or slits, narrow and high, far out of the assailants' reach, and piercing the walls without regard to symmetry — not, as Ruskin would have us believe, because irregularity was thought artistic, but because the mediæval architect, trained to the uses of necessity, knew that he must design openings that should afford no passage to the besiegers' arrows, no clue to what was going on inside the keep. But to the reader familiar with Viollet-le-Duc, or with any of the many excellent works on English domestic architecture, further details will seem superfluous. It is necessary, however, to point out that long after the conditions of life in Europe had changed, houses retained many features of the feudal period. The survival of obsolete customs which makes the study of sociology so interesting, has its parallel in the history of architecture. In the feudal countries especially, where the conflict between the great nobles and the king was of such long duration that civilization spread very slowly, architecture was proportionately slow to give up many of its feudal characteristics. In Italy, on the contrary, where one city after another succumbed to some accomplished condottiere who between his campaigns read Virgil and collected antique marbles, the rugged little republics were soon converted into brilliant courts where, life being relatively secure, social intercourse rapidly developed. This change of conditions brought with it the paved street and square, the large-windowed palaces with their great court-yards and stately open staircases, and the market-place with its loggia adorned with statues and marble seats.

Italy, in short, returned instinctively to the Roman ideal of civic life: the life of the street, the forum and the baths. These very conditions, though approaching so much nearer than feudalism to our modern civilization, in some respects make the Italian architecture of the Renaissance less serviceable as a model than the French and English styles later developed from it. The very dangers and barbarities of feudalism had fostered and preserved the idea of home as of something private, shut off from intrusion; and while the Roman ideal flowered in the great palace with its galleries, loggias and saloons, itself a kind of roofed-in forum, the French or English feudal keep became, by the same process of growth, the modern private house. The domestic architecture of the Renaissance in Italy offers but two distinctively characteristic styles of building: the palace and the villa or hunting-lodge.[1] There is nothing corresponding in interior arrangements with the French or English town house, or the *manoir* where the provincial nobles lived all the year round. The villa was a mere perch used for a few weeks of gaiety in spring or autumn; it was never a home as the French or English country-house was. There were, of course, private houses in Renaissance Italy, but these were occupied rather by shopkeepers, craftsmen, and the *bourgeoisie* than by the class which in France and England lived

---

[1] Charming as the Italian villa is, it can hardly be used in our Northern States without certain modifications, unless it is merely occupied for a few weeks in midsummer; whereas the average French or English country house built after 1600 is perfectly suited to our climate and habits. The chief features of the Italian villa are the open central *cortile* and the large saloon two stories high. An adaptation of these better suited to a cold climate is to be found in the English country houses built in the Palladian manner after its introduction by Inigo Jones. See Campbell's *Vitruvius Britannicus* for numerous examples.

ın country houses or small private hôtels. The elevations of
these small Italian houses are often admirable examples of domestic architecture, but their planning is rudimentary, and it may be
said that the characteristic tendencies of modern house-planning
were developed rather in the mezzanin or low-studded intermediate story of the Italian Renaissance palace than in the small
house of the same period.

It is a fact recognized by political economists that changes in
manners and customs, no matter under what form of government,
usually originate with the wealthy or aristocratic minority, and
are thence transmitted to the other classes. Thus the *bourgeois*
of one generation lives more like the aristocrat of a previous
generation than like his own predecessors. This rule naturally
holds good of house-planning, and it is for this reason that the
origin of modern house-planning should be sought rather in the
prince's mezzanin than in the small middle-class dwelling. The
Italian mezzanin probably originated in the habit of building
certain very high-studded saloons and of lowering the ceiling
of the adjoining rooms. This created an intermediate story, or
rather scattered intermediate rooms, which Bramante was among
the first to use in the planning of his palaces; but Bramante did
not reveal the existence of the mezzanin in his façades, and it was
not until the time of Peruzzi and his contemporaries that it became, both in plan and elevation, an accepted part of the Italian
palace. It is for this reason that the year 1500 is a convenient
point from which to date the beginning of modern house-planning; but it must be borne in mind that this date is purely arbitrary, and represents merely an imaginary line drawn between
mediæval and modern ways of living and house-planning, as
exemplified respectively, for instance, in the ducal palace of Ur-

bino, built by Luciano da Laurano about 1468, and the palace of the Massimi alle Colonne in Rome, built by Baldassare Peruzzi during the first half of the sixteenth century.

The lives of the great Italian nobles were essentially open-air lives: all was organized with a view to public pageants, ceremonies and entertainments. Domestic life was subordinated to this spectacular existence, and instead of building private houses in our sense, they built palaces, of which they set aside a portion for the use of the family. Every Italian palace has its mezzanin or private apartment; but this part of the building is now seldom seen by travellers in Italy. Not only is it usually inhabited by the owners of the palace but, its decorations being simpler than those of the *piano nobile*, or principal story, it is not thought worthy of inspection. As a matter of fact, the treatment of the mezzanin was generally most beautiful, because most suitable ; and while the Italian Renaissance palace can seldom serve as a model for a modern private house, the decoration of the mezzanin rooms is full of appropriate suggestion.

In France and England, on the other hand, private life was gradually, though slowly, developing along the lines it still follows in the present day. It is necessary to bear in mind that what we call modern civilization was a later growth in these two countries than in Italy. If this fact is insisted upon, it is only because it explains the relative unsuitability of French Renaissance or Tudor and Elizabethan architecture to modern life. In France, for instance, it was not until the Fronde was subdued and Louis XIV firmly established on the throne, that the elements which compose what we call modern life really began to combine. In fact, it might be said that the feudalism of which the Fronde was the lingering expression had its counterpart in the architecture of the period. While long familiarity with Italy was beginning to tell upon the practical side of house-planning, many obsolete details were still preserved. Even the most enthusiastic admirer of the French Renaissance would hardly maintain that the houses of that period are what we should call in the modern sense "convenient." It would be impossible for a modern family to occupy with any degree of comfort the Hôtel Voguë at Dijon, one of the best examples (as originally planned) of sixteenth-century domestic architecture in France.[1] The same objection applies to the furniture of the period. This arose from the fact that, owing to the unsettled state of the country, the landed proprietor always carried his furniture with him when he travelled from one estate to another. Furniture, in the vocabulary of the middle ages, meant something which may be transported: "Meubles sont apelez qu'on peut transporter"; — hence the lack of variety in furniture before the seventeenth century, and also its unsuitableness to modern life. Chairs and cabinets that had to be carried about on mule-back were necessarily somewhat stiff and angular in design. It is perhaps not too much to say that a comfortable chair, in our self-indulgent modern sense, did not exist before the Louis XIV armchair (see Plate IV); and the cushioned *bergère*, the ancestor of our upholstered easy-chair, cannot be traced back further than the Regency. Prior to the time of Louis XIV, the most luxurious people had to content themselves with hard straight-backed seats. The necessities of transportation permitted little variety of design, and every piece of furniture was constructed with the double purpose of being easily carried about and of being used as a trunk (see Plate I). As Havard says, "Tout meuble se traduisait par un coffre." The unvarying design of the

[1] The plan of the Hôtel Voguë has been greatly modified.

cabinets is explained by the fact that they were made to form two trunks,[1] and even the chairs and settles had hollow seats which could be packed with the owners' wardrobe (see Plate II). The king himself, when he went from one château to another, carried all his furniture with him, and it is thus not surprising that lesser people contented themselves with a few substantial chairs and cabinets, and enough arras or cloth of Douai to cover the draughty walls of their country-houses. One of Madame de Sévigné's letters gives an amusing instance of the scarceness of furniture even in the time of Louis XIV. In describing a fire in a house near her own hôtel in Paris, she says that one or two of the persons from the burning house were brought to her for shelter, because it was known in the neighborhood (at that time a rich and fashionable one) that she had *an extra bed* in the house!

It was not until the social influences of the reign of Louis XIV were fully established that modern domestic life really began. Tradition ascribes to Madame de Rambouillet a leading share in the advance in practical house-planning; but probably what she did is merely typical of the modifications which the new social conditions were everywhere producing. It is certain that at this time houses and rooms first began to be comfortable. The immense cavernous fireplaces originally meant for the roasting of beeves and the warming of a flock of frozen retainers,— "les grandes antiquailles de cheminées," as Madame de Sévigné called them,— were replaced by the compact chimney-piece of modern times. Cushioned *bergères* took the place of the throne-like seats of Louis XIII, screens kept off unwelcome draughts, Savonnerie

---

[1] Cabinets retained this shape after the transporting of furniture had ceased to be a necessity (see Plate III).

or moquette carpets covered the stone or marble floors, and grandeur gave way to luxury.[1]

English architecture having followed a line of development so similar that it need not here be traced, it remains only to examine in detail the opening proposition, namely, that modern architecture and decoration, having in many ways deviated from the paths which the experience of the past had marked out for them, can be reclaimed only by a study of the best models.

It might of course be said that to attain this end originality is more necessary than imitativeness. To this it may be replied that no lost art can be re-acquired without at least for a time going back to the methods and manner of those who formerly practised it; or the objection may be met by the question, What is originality in art? Perhaps it is easier to define what it is *not;* and this may be done by saying that it is never a wilful rejection of what have been accepted as the necessary laws of the various forms of art. Thus, in reasoning, originality lies not in discarding the necessary laws of thought, but in using them to express new intellectual conceptions; in poetry, originality consists not in discarding the necessary laws of rhythm, but in finding new rhythms within the limits of those laws. Most of the features of architecture that have persisted through various fluctuations of taste owe their preservation to the fact that they have been proved by experience to be necessary; and it will be found that none of them precludes the exercise of individual taste, any more than the acceptance of the syllogism or of the laws of rhythm prevents new thinkers and new poets from saying what has never

[1] It must be remembered that in describing the decoration of any given period, we refer to the private houses, not the royal palaces, of that period. Versailles was more splendid than any previous palace; but private houses at that date were less splendid, though far more luxurious, than during the Renaissance.

been said before.   Once this is clearly understood, it will be seen
that the supposed conflict between originality and tradition is no
conflict at all.[1]

In citing logic and poetry, those arts have been purposely
chosen of which the laws will perhaps best help to explain and
illustrate the character of architectural limitations. A building,
for whatever purpose erected, must be built in strict accordance
with the requirements of that purpose; in other words, it must
have a reason for being as it is and must be as it is for that reason.
Its decoration must harmonize with the structural limitations
(which is by no means the same thing as saying that all decoration must be structural), and from this harmony of the general
scheme of decoration with the building, and of the details of
the decoration with each other, springs the rhythm that distinguishes architecture from mere construction.   Thus all good
architecture and good decoration (which, it must never be forgotten, *is only interior architecture*) must be based on rhythm
and logic.   A house, or room, must be planned as it is because
it could not, in reason, be otherwise; must be decorated as it is
because no other decoration would harmonize as well with the
plan.

Many of the most popular features in modern house-planning
and decoration will not be found to stand this double test.   Often
(as will be shown further on) they are merely survivals of earlier
social conditions, and have been preserved in obedience to that
instinct that makes people cling to so many customs the

[1] " Si l'on dispose un édifice d'une manière convenable à l'usage auquel on le
destine, ne différera-t-il pas sensiblement d'un autre édifice destiné à un autre usage ?
N'aura-t-il pas naturellement un caractère, et, qui plus est, son caractère propre ? "
J. L. N. Durand. *Précis des Leçons d'Architecture données à l'École Royale Polytechnique.* Paris, 1823.

III FRENCH ARMOIRE

XVI CENTURY

The Metropolitan Museum of Art, Rogers Fund, 1925

IV   FRENCH SOFA AND ARMCHAIR

FROM THE CHÂTEAU DE BERCY. LOUIS XIV PERIOD

meaning of which is lost. In other cases they have been revived
by the archæologizing spirit which is so characteristic of the
present time, and which so often leads its possessors to think
that a thing must be beautiful because it is old and appropriate
because it is beautiful.

But since the beauty of all such features depends on their appropriateness, they may in every case be replaced by a more
suitable form of treatment without loss to the general effect of
house or room. It is this which makes it important that each
room (or, better still, all the rooms) in a house should receive the
same style of decoration. To some people this may seem as
meaningless a piece of archaism as the habit of using obsolete
fragments of planning or decoration; but such is not the case.
It must not be forgotten, in discussing the question of reproducing certain styles, that the essence of a style lies not in its use of
ornament, but in its handling of proportion. Structure conditions
ornament, not ornament structure. That is, a room with unsuit-
ably proportioned openings, wall-spaces and cornice might receive a surface application of Louis XV or Louis XVI ornament
and not represent either of those styles of decoration; whereas a
room constructed according to the laws of proportion accepted in
one or the other of those periods, in spite of a surface application
of decorative detail widely different in character,— say Roman-
esque or Gothic,— would yet maintain its distinctive style, because the detail, in conforming with the laws of proportion
governing the structure of the room, must necessarily conform
with its style. In other words, decoration is always subservient
to proportion; and a room, whatever its decoration may be, must
represent the style to which its proportions belong. The less
cannot include the greater. Unfortunately it is usually by orna-

mental details, rather than by proportion, that people distinguish one style from another. To many persons, garlands, bow-knots, quivers, and a great deal of gilding represent the Louis XVI style; if they object to these, they condemn the style. To an architect familiar with the subject the same style means something absolutely different. He knows that a Louis XVI room may exist without any of these or similar characteristics; and he often deprecates their use as representing the cheaper and more trivial effects of the period, and those that have most helped to vulgarize it. In fact, in nine cases out of ten his use of them is a concession to the client who, having asked for a Louis XVI room, would not know he had got it were these details left out.[1]

Another thing which has perhaps contributed to make people distrustful of "styles" is the garbled form in which they are presented by some architects. After a period of eclecticism that has lasted long enough to make architects and decorators lose their traditional habits of design, there has arisen a sudden demand for "style." It necessarily follows that only the most competent are ready to respond to this unexpected summons. Much has to be relearned, still more to be unlearned. The essence of the great styles lay in proportion and the science of proportion is not to be acquired in a day. In fact, in such matters the cultivated layman, whether or not he has any special familiarity with the different schools of architecture, is often a better judge than the half-educated architect. It is no wonder that people of taste are disconcerted by the so-called "colonial" houses where stair-rails are used as roof-balustrades and mantel-

---

[1] It must not be forgotten that the so-called "styles" of Louis XIV, Louis XV and Louis XVI were, in fact, only the gradual development of one organic style, and hence differed only in the superficial use of ornament.

friezes as exterior entablatures, or by Louis XV rooms where the wavy movement which, in the best rococo, was always an ornamental incident and never broke up the main lines of the design, is suffered to run riot through the whole treatment of the walls, so that the bewildered eye seeks in vain for a straight line amid the whirl of incoherent curves.

To conform to a style, then, is to accept those rules of proportion which the artistic experience of centuries has established as the best, while within those limits allowing free scope to the individual requirements which must inevitably modify every house or room adapted to the use and convenience of its occupants.

There is one thing more to be said in defence of conformity to style; and that is, the difficulty of getting rid of style. Strive as we may for originality, we are hampered at every turn by an artistic tradition of over two thousand years. Does any but the most inexperienced architect really think that he can ever rid himself of such an inheritance? He may mutilate or misapply the component parts of his design, but he cannot originate a whole new architectural alphabet. The chances are that he will not find it easy to invent one wholly new moulding.

The styles especially suited to modern life have already been roughly indicated as those prevailing in Italy since 1500, in France from the time of Louis XIV, and in England since the introduction of the Italian manner by Inigo Jones; and as the French and English styles are perhaps more familiar to the general reader, the examples given will usually be drawn from these. Supposing the argument in favor of these styles to have been accepted, at least as a working hypothesis, it must be explained why, in each room, the decoration and furniture should harmonize. Most people will admit the necessity of harmonizing the colors in a room, because a feeling for color is more general than a feeling for form; but in reality the latter is the more important in decoration, and it is the feeling for form, and not any archæological affectation, which makes the best decorators insist upon the necessity of keeping to the same style of furniture and decoration. Thus the massive dimensions and heavy panelling of a seventeenth-century room would dwarf a set of eighteenth-century furniture; and the wavy, capricious movement of Louis XV decoration would make the austere yet delicate lines of Adam furniture look stiff and mean.

Many persons object not only to any attempt at uniformity of style, but to the use of any recognized style in the decoration of a room. They characterize it, according to their individual views, as "servile," "formal," or "pretentious."

It has already been suggested that to conform within rational limits to a given style is no more servile than to pay one's taxes or to write according to the rules of grammar. As to the accusations of formality and pretentiousness (which are more often made in America than elsewhere), they may probably be explained by the fact that most Americans necessarily form their idea of the great European styles from public buildings and palaces. Certainly, if an architect were to propose to his client to decorate a room in a moderate-sized house in the Louis XIV style, and if the client had formed his idea of that style from the state apartments in the palace at Versailles, he would be justified in rejecting the proposed treatment as absolutely unsuitable to modern private life; whereas the architect who had gone somewhat more deeply into the subject might have singled out the style as eminently suitable, having in mind one of the simple panelled rooms, with tall

V   ROOM IN THE GRAND TRIANON

VERSAILLES

(EXAMPLE OF SIMPLE LOUIS XIV DECORATION)

VI   FRENCH ARMCHAIR

LOUIS XV PERIOD

The Metropolitan Museum of Art, Gift of J. Pierpont Morgan, 1906

windows, a dignified fireplace, large tables and comfortable arm-chairs, which were to be found in the private houses of the same period (see Plate V). It is the old story of the two knights fighting about the color of the shield. Both architect and client would be right, but they would be looking at the different sides of the question. As a matter of fact, the bed-rooms, sitting-rooms, libraries and other private apartments in the smaller dwelling-houses built in Europe between 1650 and 1800 were far simpler, less pretentious and more practical in treatment than those in the average modern house.

It is therefore hoped that the antagonists of "style," when they are shown that to follow a certain style is not to sacrifice either convenience or imagination, but to give more latitude to both, will withdraw an opposition which seems to be based on a mis-apprehension of facts.

Hitherto architecture and decoration have been spoken of as one, as in any well-designed house they ought to be. Indeed, it is one of the numerous disadvantages of the present use of styles, that unless the architect who has built the house also decorates it, the most hopeless discord is apt to result. This was otherwise before our present desire for variety had thrown architects, decorators, and workmen out of the regular routine of their business. Before 1800 the decorator called upon to treat the interior of a house invariably found a suitable background prepared for his work, while much in the way of detail was intrusted to the workmen, who were trained in certain traditions instead of being called upon to carry out in each new house the vagaries of a different designer.

But it is with the decorator's work alone that these pages are concerned, and the above digression is intended to explain why his task is now so difficult, and why his results are so often unsatisfactory to himself as well as to his clients.   The decorator of the present day may be compared to a person who is called upon to write a letter in the English language, but is ordered, in so doing, to conform to the Chinese or Egyptian rules of grammar, or possibly to both together.

By the use of a little common sense and a reasonable conformity to those traditions of design which have been tested by generations of architects, it is possible to produce great variety in the decoration of rooms without losing sight of the purpose for which they are intended.   Indeed, the more closely this purpose is kept in view, and the more clearly it is expressed in all the details of each room, the more pleasing that room will be, so that it is easy to make a room with tinted walls, deal furniture and dimity curtains more beautiful, because more logical and more harmonious, than a ball-room lined with gold and marbles, in which the laws of rhythm and logic have been ignored.

II

ROOMS IN GENERAL

BEFORE beginning to decorate a room it is essential to consider for what purpose the room is to be used. It is not enough to ticket it with some such general designation as "library," "drawing-room," or "den." The individual tastes and habits of the people who are to occupy it must be taken into account; it must be not "a library," or "a drawing-room," but the library or the drawing-room best suited to the master or mistress of the house which is being decorated. Individuality in house-furnishing has seldom been more harped upon than at the present time. That cheap originality which finds expression in putting things to uses for which they were not intended is often confounded with individuality; whereas the latter consists not in an attempt to be different from other people at the cost of comfort, but in the desire to be comfortable in one's own way, even though it be the way of a monotonously large majority. It seems easier to most people to arrange a room like some one else's than to analyze and express their own needs. Men, in these matters, are less exacting than women, because their demands, besides being simpler, are uncomplicated by the feminine tendency to want things because other people have them, rather than to have things because they are wanted.

But it must never be forgotten that every one is unconsciously tyrannized over by the wants of others,— the wants of dead and gone predecessors, who have an inconvenient way of thrusting their different habits and tastes across the current of later existences.   The unsatisfactory relations of some people with their rooms are often to be explained in this way.   They have still in their blood the traditional uses to which these rooms were put in times quite different from the present.   It is only an unconscious extension of the conscious habit which old-fashioned people have of clinging to their parents' way of living.   The difficulty of reconciling these instincts with our own comfort and convenience, and the various compromises to which they lead in the arrangement of our rooms, will be more fully dealt with in the following chapters.   To go to the opposite extreme and discard things because they are old-fashioned is equally unreasonable.   The golden mean lies in trying to arrange our houses with a view to our own comfort and convenience; and it will be found that the more closely we follow this rule the easier our rooms will be to furnish and the pleasanter to live in.

People whose attention has never been specially called to the *raison d'être* of house-furnishing sometimes conclude that because a thing is unusual it is artistic, or rather that through some occult process the most ordinary things become artistic by being used in an unusual manner; while others, warned by the visible results of this theory of furnishing, infer that everything artistic is unpractical.   In the Anglo-Saxon mind beauty is not spontaneously born of material wants, as it is with the Latin races.   We have to *make* things beautiful; they do not grow so of themselves.   The necessity of making this effort has caused many people to put aside the whole problem of beauty and fitness in household decoration as something mysterious and incomprehensible to the uninitiated. The architect and decorator are often aware that they are regarded by their clients as the possessors of some strange craft like black magic or astrology.

This fatalistic attitude has complicated the simple and intelligible process of house-furnishing, and has produced much of the discomfort which causes so many rooms to be shunned by everybody in the house, in spite (or rather because) of all the money and ingenuity expended on their arrangement. Yet to penetrate the mystery of house-furnishing it is only necessary to analyze one satisfactory room and to notice wherein its charm lies. To the fastidious eye it will, of course, be found in fitness of proportion, in the proper use of each moulding and in the harmony of all the decorative processes ; and even to those who think themselves indifferent to such detail, much of the sense of restfulness and comfort produced by certain rooms depends on the due adjustment of their fundamental parts. Different rooms minister to different wants and while a room may be made very livable without satisfying any but the material requirements of its inmates it is evident that the perfect room should combine these qualities with what corresponds to them in a higher order of needs. At present, however, the subject deals only with the material livableness of a room, and this will generally be found to consist in the position of the doors and fireplace, the accessibility of the windows, the arrangement of the furniture, the privacy of the room and the absence of the superfluous.

The position of doors and fireplace, though the subject comes properly under the head of house-planning, may be included in this summary, because in rearranging a room it is often possible to change its openings, or at any rate, in the case of doors, to modify their dimensions.

The fireplace must be the focus of every rational scheme of arrangement. Nothing is so dreary, so hopeless to deal with, as a room in which the fireplace occupies a narrow space between two doors, so that it is impossible to sit about the hearth.[1] Next in importance come the windows. In town houses especially, where there is so little light that every ray is precious to the reader or worker, window-space is invaluable. Yet in few rooms are the windows easy of approach, free from useless draperies and provided with easy-chairs so placed that the light falls properly on the occupant's work.

It is no exaggeration to say that many houses are deserted by the men of the family for lack of those simple comforts which they find at their clubs: windows unobscured by layers of muslin, a fireplace surrounded by easy-chairs and protected from draughts, well-appointed writing-tables and files of papers and magazines. Who cannot call to mind the dreary drawing-room, in small town houses the only possible point of reunion for the family, but too often, in consequence of its exquisite discomfort, of no more use as a meeting-place than the vestibule or the cellar? The windows in this kind of room are invariably supplied with two sets of muslin curtains, one hanging against the panes, the other fulfilling the supererogatory duty of hanging against the former; then come the heavy stuff curtains, so draped as to cut off the upper light of the windows by day, while it is impossible to drop them at night: curtains that have thus ceased to serve the purpose for which they exist. Close to the curtains stands

[1] There is no objection to putting a fireplace between two doors, provided both doors be at least six feet from the chimney.

VII   FRENCH BERGÈRE

LOUIS XVI PERIOD

The Metropolitan Museum of Art, Gift of the Samuel H. Kress Foundation

VIII   FRENCH BERGÈRE

LOUIS XVI PERIOD

The Metropolitan Museum of Art, Gift of Ann Payne Blumenthal, 1941

the inevitable lamp or jardinière, and the wall-space between the two windows, where a writing-table might be put, is generally taken up by a cabinet or console, surmounted by a picture made invisible by the dark shadow of the hangings. The writing-table might find place against the side-wall near either window ; but these spaces are usually sacred to the piano and to that modern futility, the silver-table. Thus of necessity the writing-table is either banished or put in some dark corner, where it is little wonder that the ink dries unused and a vase of flowers grows in the middle of the blotting-pad.

The hearth should be the place about which people gather; but the mantelpiece in the average American house, being ugly, is usually covered with inflammable draperies; the fire is, in consequence, rarely lit, and no one cares to sit about a fireless hearth. Besides, on the opposite side of the room is a gap in the wall eight or ten feet wide, opening directly upon the hall, and exposing what should be the most private part of the room to the scrutiny of messengers, servants and visitors. This opening is sometimes provided with doors; but these, as a rule, are either slid into the wall or are unhung and replaced by a curtain through which every word spoken in the room must necessarily pass. In such a room it matters very little how the rest of the furniture is arranged, since it is certain that no one will ever sit in it except the luckless visitor who has no other refuge.

Even the visitor might be thought entitled to the solace of a few books; but as all the tables in the room are littered with knick-knacks, it is difficult for the most philanthropic hostess to provide even this slight alleviation.

When the town-house is built on the basement plan, and the drawing-room or parlor is up-stairs, the family, to escape from its discomforts, habitually take refuge in the small room opening off the hall on the ground floor; so that instead of sitting in a room twenty or twenty-five feet wide, they are packed into one less than half that size and exposed to the frequent intrusions from which, in basement houses, the drawing-room is free. But too often even the "little room down-stairs" is arranged less like a sitting-room in a private house than a waiting-room at a fashionable doctor's or dentist's. It has the inevitable yawning gap in the wall, giving on the hall close to the front door, and is either the refuge of the ugliest and most uncomfortable furniture in the house, or, even if furnished with taste, is arranged with so little regard to comfort that one might as well make it part of the hall, as is often done in rearranging old houses. This habit of sacrificing a useful room to the useless widening of the hall is indeed the natural outcome of furnishing rooms of this kind in so unpractical a way that their real usefulness has ceased to be apparent. The science of restoring wasted rooms to their proper uses is one of the most important and least understood branches of house-furnishing.

Privacy would seem to be one of the first requisites of civilized life, yet it is only necessary to observe the planning and arrangement of the average house to see how little this need is recognized. Each room in a house has its individual uses: some are made to sleep in, others are for dressing, eating, study, or conversation; but whatever the uses of a room, they are seriously interfered with if it be not preserved as a small world by itself. If the drawing-room be a part of the hall and the library a part of the drawing-room, all three will be equally unfitted to serve their special purpose. The indifference to privacy which has sprung up in modern times, and which in France, for instance, has given rise to the grotesque conceit of putting sheets of plate-glass between two rooms, and of replacing doorways by openings fifteen feet wide, is of complex origin.   It is probably due in part to the fact that many houses are built and decorated by people unfamiliar with the habits of those for whom they are building. It may be that architect and decorator live in a simpler manner than their clients, and are therefore ready to sacrifice a kind of comfort of which they do not feel the need to the "effects" obtainable by vast openings and extended "vistas."   To the untrained observer size often appeals more than proportion and costliness than suitability.   In a handsome house such an observer is attracted rather by the ornamental detail than by the underlying purpose of planning and decoration.   He sees the beauty of the detail, but not its relation to the whole.   He therefore regards it as elegant but useless; and his next step is to infer that there is an inherent elegance in what is useless.

Before beginning to decorate a house it is necessary to make a prolonged and careful study of its plan and elevations, both as a whole and in detail.   The component parts of an undecorated room are its floor, ceiling, wall-spaces and openings.   The openings consist of the doors, windows and fireplace ; and of these, as has already been pointed out, the fireplace is the most important in the general scheme of decoration.

No room can be satisfactory unless its openings are properly placed and proportioned, and the decorator's task is much easier if he has also been the architect of the house he is employed to decorate ; but as this seldom happens his ingenuity is frequently taxed to produce a good design upon the background of a faulty and illogical structure.   Much may be done to overcome this difficulty by making slight changes in the proportions of the openings; and the skilful decorator, before applying his scheme of decoration, will do all that he can to correct the fundamental lines of the room.   But the result is seldom so successful as if he had built the room, and those who employ different people to build and decorate their houses should at least try to select an architect and a decorator trained in the same school of composition, so that they may come to some understanding with regard to the general harmony of their work.

In deciding upon a scheme of decoration, it is necessary to keep in mind the relation of furniture to ornament, and of the room as a whole to other rooms in the house.   As in a small house a very large room dwarfs all the others, so a room decorated in a very rich manner will make the simplicity of those about it look mean.   Every house should be decorated according to a carefully graduated scale of ornamentation culminating in the most important room of the house ; but this plan must be carried out with such due sense of the relation of the rooms to each other that there shall be no violent break in the continuity of treatment.   If a white-and-gold drawing-room opens on a hall with a Brussels carpet and papered walls, the drawing-room will look too fine and the hall mean.

In the furnishing of each room the same rule should be as carefully observed.   The simplest and most cheaply furnished room (provided the furniture be good of its kind, and the walls and carpet unobjectionable in color) will be more pleasing to the fastidious eye than one in which gilded consoles and cabinets of buhl stand side by side with cheap machine-made furniture, and delicate old marquetry tables are covered with trashy china ornaments.

It is, of course, not always possible to refurnish a room when it is redecorated.   Many people must content themselves with using their old furniture, no matter how ugly and ill-assorted it may be; and it is the decorator's business to see that his background helps the furniture to look its best. It is a mistake to think that because the furniture of a room is inappropriate or ugly a good background will bring out these defects. It will, on the contrary, be a relief to the eye to escape from the bad lines of the furniture to the good lines of the walls ; and should the opportunity to purchase new furniture ever come, there will be a suitable background ready to show it to the best advantage.

Most rooms contain a mixture of good, bad, and indifferent furniture. It is best to adapt the decorative treatment to the best pieces and to discard those which are in bad taste, replacing them, if necessary, by willow chairs and stained deal tables until it is possible to buy something better. When the room is to be refurnished as well as redecorated the client often makes his purchases without regard to the decoration. Besides being an injustice to the decorator, inasmuch as it makes it impossible for him to harmonize his decoration with the furniture, this generally produces a result unsatisfactory to the owner of the house. Neither decoration nor furniture, however good of its kind, can look its best unless each is chosen with reference to the other. It is therefore necessary that the decorator, before planning his treatment of a room, should be told what it is to contain. If a gilt set is put in a room the walls of which are treated in low relief and painted white, the high lights of the gilding will destroy the delicate values of the mouldings, and the walls, at a little distance, will look like flat expanses of whitewashed plaster.

When a room is to be furnished and decorated at the smallest possible cost, it must be remembered that the comfort of its occupants depends more on the nature of the furniture than of the wall-decorations or carpet. In a living-room of this kind it is best to tint the walls and put a cheerful drugget on the floor, keeping as much money as possible for the purchase of comfortable chairs and sofas and substantial tables. If little can be spent in buying furniture, willow arm-chairs[1] with denim cushions and solid tables with stained legs and covers of denim or corduroy will be more satisfactory than the "parlor suit" turned out in thousands by the manufacturer of cheap furniture, or the pseudo-Georgian or pseudo-Empire of the dealer in "high-grade goods." Plain bookcases may be made of deal, painted or stained; and a room treated in this way, with a uniform color on the wall, and plenty of lamps and books, is sure to be comfortable and can never be vulgar.

It is to be regretted that, in this country and in England, it should be almost impossible to buy plain but well-designed and substantial furniture. Nothing can exceed the ugliness of the current designs: the bedsteads with towering head-boards fretted by the versatile jig-saw; the "bedroom suits" of "mahoganized" cherry, bird's-eye maple, or some other crude-colored wood; the tables with meaninglessly turned legs; the "Empire" chairs and consoles stuck over with ornaments of cast bronze washed in liquid gilding; and, worst of all, the supposed "Colonial" furniture, that unworthy travesty of a plain and dignified style. All this showy stuff has been produced in answer to the increasing demand for cheap "effects" in place of unobtrusive merit in material and design; but now that an appreciation of better things in architecture is becoming more general, it is to be hoped that the "artistic" furniture disfiguring so many of our shop-windows will no longer find a market.

[1] Not rattan, as the models are too bad.

There is no lack of models for manufacturers to copy, if their customers will but demand what is good. France and England, in the eighteenth century, excelled in the making of plain, inexpensive furniture of walnut, mahogany, or painted beechwood (see Plates VII–X). Simple in shape and substantial in construction, this kind of furniture was never tricked out with moulded bronzes and machine-made carving, or covered with liquid gilding, but depended for its effect upon the solid qualities of good material, good design and good workmanship. The eighteenth-century cabinet-maker did not attempt cheap copies of costly furniture; the common sense of his patrons would have resented such a perversion of taste. Were the modern public as fastidious, it would soon be easy to buy good furniture for a moderate price; but until people recognize the essential vulgarity of the pinchbeck article flooding our shops and overflowing upon our sidewalks, manufacturers will continue to offer such wares in preference to better but less showy designs.

The worst defects of the furniture now made in America are due to an Athenian thirst for novelty, not always regulated by an Athenian sense of fitness. No sooner is it known that beautiful furniture was made in the time of Marie-Antoinette than an epidemic of supposed "Marie-Antoinette" rooms breaks out over the whole country. Neither purchaser nor manufacturer has stopped to inquire wherein the essentials of the style consist. They know that the rooms of the period were usually painted in light colors, and that the furniture (in palaces) was often gilt and covered with brocade; and it is taken for granted that plenty of white paint, a pale wall-paper with bow-knots, and fragile chairs dipped in liquid gilding and covered with a flowered silk-and-cotton material, must inevitably produce a "Marie-An-

toinette" room.   According to the creed of the modern manufacturer, you have only to combine certain "goods" to obtain
a certain style.

This quest of artistic novelties would be encouraging were it
based on the desire for something better, rather than for something
merely different.   The tendency to dash from one style to another, without stopping to analyze the intrinsic qualities of any,
has defeated the efforts of those who have tried to teach the true
principles of furniture-designing by a return to the best models.
If people will buy the stuff now offered them as Empire, Sheraton
or Louis XVI, the manufacturer is not to blame for making it.
It is not the maker but the purchaser who sets the standard; and
there will never be any general supply of better furniture until
people take time to study the subject, and find out wherein lies
the radical unfitness of what now contents them.

Until this golden age arrives the householder who cannot afford
to buy old pieces, or to have old models copied by a skilled
cabinet-maker, had better restrict himself to the plainest of furniture, relying for the embellishment of his room upon good
bookbindings and one or two old porcelain vases for his lamps.

Concerning the difficult question of color, it is safe to say that
the fewer the colors used in a room, the more pleasing and restful
the result will be.   A multiplicity of colors produces the same
effect as a number of voices talking at the same time.   The voices
may not be discordant, but continuous chatter is fatiguing in the
long run.   Each room should speak with but one voice : it should
contain one color, which at once and unmistakably asserts its
predominance, in obedience to the rule that where there is a
division of parts one part shall visibly prevail over all the others.

To attain this result, it is best to use the same color and, if

IX FRENCH SOFA

LOUIS XV PERIOD

(TAPESTRY DESIGNED BY BOUCHER)

X FRENCH MARQUETRY AND ORMOLU
MECHANICAL TABLE

LOUIS XVI PERIOD

The Metropolitan Museum of Art, Rogers Fund, 1933

possible, the same material, for curtains and chair-coverings. This produces an impression of unity and gives an air of spaciousness to the room. When the walls are simply panelled in oak or walnut, or are painted in some neutral tones, such as gray and white, the carpet may contrast in color with the curtains and chair-coverings. For instance, in an oak-panelled room crimson curtains and chair-coverings may be used with a dull green carpet, or with one of dark blue patterned in subdued tints; or the color-scheme may be reversed, and green hangings and chair-coverings combined with a plain crimson carpet.

Where the walls are covered with tapestry, or hung with a large number of pictures, or, in short, are so treated that they present a variety of colors, it is best that curtains, chair-coverings and carpet should all be of one color and without pattern. Graduated shades oᵢ the same color should almost always be avoided; theoretically they seem harmonious, but in reality the light shades look faded in proximity with the darker ones. Though it is well, as a rule, that carpet and hangings should match, exception must always be made in favor of a really fine old Eastern rug. The tints of such rugs are too subdued, too subtly harmonized by time, to clash with any colors the room may contain; but those who cannot cover their floors in this way will do well to use carpets of uniform tint, rather than the gaudy rugs now made in the East. The modern red and green Smyrna or Turkey carpet is an exception. Where the furniture is dark and substantial, and the predominating color is a strong green or crimson, such a carpet is always suitable. These Smyrna carpets are usually well designed; and if their colors be restricted to red and green, with small admixture of dark blue, they harmonize with almost any style of decoration. It is well, as a rule, to shun the decorative schemes concocted by the writers who supply our newspapers with hints for "artistic interiors." The use of such poetic adjectives as jonquil-yellow, willow-green, shell-pink, or ashes-of-roses, gives to these descriptions of the "unique boudoir" or "ideal summer room" a charm which the reality would probably not possess. The arrangements suggested are usually cheap devices based upon the mistaken idea that defects in structure or design may be remedied by an overlaying of color or ornament. This theory often leads to the spending of much more money than would have been required to make one or two changes in the plan of the room, and the result is never satisfactory to the fastidious.

There are but two ways of dealing with a room which is fundamentally ugly: one is to accept it, and the other is courageously to correct its ugliness. Half-way remedies are a waste of money and serve rather to call attention to the defects of the room than to conceal them.

III

WALLS

PROPORTION is the good breeding of architecture. It is that something, indefinable to the unprofessional eye, which gives repose and distinction to a room: in its origin a matter of nice mathematical calculation, of scientific adjustment of voids and masses, but in its effects as intangible as that all-pervading essence which the ancients called the soul.

It is not proposed to enter here into a technical discussion of the delicate problem of proportion. The decorator, with whom this book is chiefly concerned, is generally not consulted until the house that he is to decorate has been built—and built, in all probability, quite without reference to the interior treatment it is destined to receive. All he can hope to do is, by slight modifications here and there in the dimensions or position of the openings, to re-establish that harmony of parts so frequently disregarded in modern house-planning. It often happens, however, that the decorator's desire to make these slight changes, upon which the success of his whole scheme depends, is a source of perplexity and distress to his bewildered client, who sees in it merely the inclination to find fault with another's work. Nothing can be more natural than this attitude on the part of the client. How is he to decide between the architect, who has possibly disregarded in some measure the claims of symmetry and proportion in planning the interior of the house, and the decorator who insists upon those claims without being able to justify his demands by any explanation comprehensible to the unprofessional? It is inevitable that the decorator, who comes last, should fare worse, especially as he makes his appearance at a time when contractors' bills are pouring in, and the proposition to move a mantelpiece or change the dimensions of a door opens fresh vistas of expense to the client's terrified imagination.

Undoubtedly these difficulties have diminished in the last few years. Architects are turning anew to the lost tradition of symmetry and to a scientific study of the relation between voids and masses, and the decorator's task has become correspondingly easier. Still, there are many cases where his work is complicated by some trifling obstacle, the removal of which the client opposes only because he cannot in imagination foresee the improvement which would follow. If the client permits the change to be made, he has no difficulty in appreciating the result: he cannot see it in advance.

A few words from Isaac Ware's admirable chapter on "The Origin of Proportions in the Orders"[1] may serve to show the importance of proportion in all schemes of decoration, and the necessity of conforming to certain rules that may at first appear both arbitrary and incomprehensible.

" An architect of genius," Ware writes (alluding to the latitude which the ancients allowed themselves in using the orders), " will think himself happy, in designing a building that is to be enriched with the Doric order, that he has all the latitude between two and a half and seventeen for the projecture of its capital; that he can

---

[1] *A Complete Body of Architecture,* Book II, chap. iii.

proportion this projecture to the general idea of his building any-
where between these extremes and show his authority. This is
an happiness to the person of real genius; . . . but as all architects are not, nor can be expected to be, of this stamp, it is needful
some standard should be established, founded upon what a good
taste shall most admire in the antique, and fixed as a model from
which to work, or as a test to which we may have recourse in
disputes and controversies."

If to these words be added his happy definition of the sense of
proportion as "fancy under the restraint and conduct of judgment," and his closing caution that "it is mean in the undertaker
of a great work to copy strictly, and it is dangerous to give a
loose to fancy *without a perfect knowledge how far a variation
may be justified,"* the unprofessional reader may form some idea
of the importance of proportion and of the necessity for observing
its rules.

If proportion is the good breeding of architecture, symmetry,
or the answering of one part to another, may be defined as the
sanity of decoration. The desire for symmetry, for balance, for
rhythm in form as well as in sound, is one of the most inveterate
of human instincts. Yet for years Anglo-Saxons have been taught
that to pay any regard to symmetry in architecture or decoration
is to truckle to one of the meanest forms of artistic hypocrisy.
The master who has taught this strange creed, in words magical
enough to win acceptance for any doctrine, has also revealed to
his generation so many of the forgotten beauties of early art that
it is hard to dispute his principles of æsthetics. As a guide
through the byways of art, Mr. Ruskin is entitled to the reverence
and gratitude of all; but as a logical exponent of the causes and
effects of the beauty he discovers, his authority is certainly open

to question. For years he has spent the full force of his un-matched prose in denouncing the enormity of putting a door or a window in a certain place in order that it may correspond to an-other ; nor has he scrupled to declare to the victims of this prac-tice that it leads to abysses of moral as well as of artistic degradation.

Time has taken the terror from these threats and architects are beginning to see that a regard for external symmetry, far from interfering with the requirements of house-planning, tends to produce a better, because a more carefully studied, plan, as well as a more convenient distribution of wall-space; but in the lay mind there still lingers not only a vague association between out-ward symmetry and interior discomfort, between a well-balanced façade and badly distributed rooms, but a still vaguer notion that regard for symmetry indicates poverty of invention, lack of in-genuity and weak subservience to a meaningless form.

What the instinct for symmetry means, philosophers may be left to explain; but that it does exist, that it means something, and that it is most strongly developed in those races which have reached the highest artistic civilization, must be acknowledged by all students of sociology. It is, therefore, not superfluous to point out that, in interior decoration as well as in architecture, a regard for symmetry, besides satisfying a legitimate artistic requirement, tends to make the average room not only easier to furnish, but more comfortable to live in.

As the effect produced by a room depends chiefly upon the distribution of its openings, it will be well to begin by consider-ing the treatment of the walls. It has already been said that the decorator can often improve a room, not only from the artistic point of view, but as regards the comfort of its inmates, by

XI   DRAWING-ROOM AT 44 BERKELEY SQUARE, LONDON

XVIII CENTURY. WILLIAM KENT, ARCHITECT

Sydney W. Newbery

XII GALLERY OF THE MONTHS

DUCAL PALACE, MANTUA.

John Barrington Bayley

making some slight change in the position of its openings. Take, for instance, a library in which it is necessary to put the two principal bookcases one on each side of a door or fireplace. If this opening is in the *centre* of one side of the room, the wall-decorations may be made to balance, and the bookcases may be of the same width,— an arrangement which will give to the room an air of spaciousness and repose. Should the wall-spaces on either side of the opening be of unequal extent, both decorations and book-cases must be modified in size and design; and not only does the problem become more difficult, but the result, because neces-sarily less simple, is certain to be less satisfactory. Sometimes, on the other hand, convenience is sacrificed to symmetry; and in such cases it is the decorator's business to remedy this defect, while preserving to the eye the aspect of symmetry. A long narrow room may be taken as an example. If the fireplace is in the centre of one of the long sides of the room, with a door di-rectly opposite, the hearth will be without privacy and the room virtually divided into two parts, since, in a narrow room, no one cares to sit in a line with the doorway. This division of the room makes it more difficult to furnish and less comfortable to live in, besides wasting all the floor-space between the chimney and the door. One way of overcoming the difficulty is to move the door some distance down the long side of the room, so that the space about the fireplace is no longer a thoroughfare, and the privacy of the greater part of the room is preserved, even if the door be left open. The removal of the door from the centre of one side of the room having disturbed the equilibrium of the openings, this equi-librium may be restored by placing in a line with the door, at the other end of the same side-wall, a piece of furniture correspond-ing as nearly as possible in height and width to the door. This will satisfy the eye, which in matters of symmetry demands, not absolute similarity of detail, but merely correspondence of outline and dimensions.

It is idle to multiply examples of the various ways in which such readjustments of the openings may increase the comfort and beauty of a room. Every problem in house decoration demands a slightly different application of the same general principles, and the foregoing instances are intended only to show how much depends upon the placing of openings and how reasonable is the decorator's claim to have a share in planning the background upon which his effects are to be produced.

It may surprise those whose attention has not been turned to such matters to be told that in all but the most cheaply constructed houses the interior walls are invariably treated as an order. In all houses, even of the poorest kind, the walls of the rooms are finished by a plain projecting board adjoining the floor, surmounted by one or more mouldings. This base, as it is called, is nothing more nor less than the part of an order between shaft and floor, or shaft and pedestal, as the case may be. If it be next remarked that the upper part of the wall, adjoining the ceiling, is invariably finished by a moulded projection corresponding with the crowning member of an order, it will be clear that the shaft, with its capital, has simply been omitted, or that the uniform wall-space between the base and cornice has been regarded as replacing it. In rooms of a certain height and importance the column or pilaster is frequently restored to its proper place between base and cornice; but where such treatment is too monumental for the dimensions of the room, the main lines of the wall-space should none the less be regarded as distinctly architectural, and the decoration applied should be subordinate to the implied existence of an order. (For the application of an order to walls, see Plates XLII and L.)

Where the shafts are omitted, the eye undoubtedly feels a lack of continuity in the treatment: the cornice seems to hang in air and the effect produced is unsatisfactory. This is obviated by the use of panelling, the vertical lines carried up at intervals from base to cornice satisfying the need for some visible connection between the upper and lower members of the order. Moreover, if the lines of the openings are carried up to the cornice (as they are in all well-designed schemes of decoration), the openings may be considered as intercolumniations and the intermediate wall-spaces as the shafts or piers supporting the cornice.

In well-finished rooms the order is usually imagined as resting, not on the floor, but on pedestals, or rather on a continuous pedestal. This continuous pedestal, or "dado" as it is usually called, is represented by a plinth surmounted by mouldings, by an intermediate member often decorated with tablets or sunk panels with moulded margins, and by a cornice. The use of the dado raises the chief wall-decoration of the room to a level with the eye and prevents its being interrupted or concealed by the furniture which may be placed against the walls. This fact makes it clear that in all well-designed rooms there should be a dado about two and a half feet high. If lower than this, it does not serve its purpose of raising the wall-decoration to a line above the furniture; while the high dado often seen in modern American rooms throws all the rest of the panelling out of scale and loses its own significance as the pedestal supporting an order.

In rooms of the sixteenth and seventeenth centuries, when little furniture was used, the dado was often richly ornamented, being sometimes painted with delicate arabesques corresponding with those on the doors and inside shutters. As rooms grew smaller and the quantity of furniture increased so much that the dado was almost concealed, the treatment of the latter was wisely simplified, being reduced, as a rule, to sunk panels and a few strongly marked mouldings. The decorator cannot do better than plan the ornamentation of his dado according to the amount of furniture to be placed against the walls. In corridor or ante-chamber, or in a ball-room, the dado may receive a more elaborate treatment than is necessary in a library or drawing-room, where probably much less of it will be seen. It was not unusual, in the decoration of lobbies and corridors in old French and Italian houses, to omit the dado entirely if an order was used, thus bringing the wall-decoration down to the base-board; but this was done only in rooms or passage-ways not meant to contain any furniture.

The three noblest forms of wall-decoration are fresco-painting, panelling, and tapestry hangings. In the best period of decoration all three were regarded as subordinate to the architectural lines of the room. The Italian fresco-painters, from Giotto to Tiepolo, never lost sight of the interrelation between painting and architecture. It matters not if the connection between base and cornice be maintained by actual pilasters or mouldings, or by their painted or woven imitations. The line, and not the substance, is what the eye demands. It is a curious perversion of artistic laws that has led certain critics to denounce painted architecture or woven mouldings. As in imaginative literature the author may present to his reader as possible anything that he has the talent to make the reader accept, so in decorative art the artist is justified in presenting to the eye whatever his skill can devise to satisfy its requirements; nor is there any insincerity in this proceeding. Decorative art is not an exact science. The decorator is not a chemist or a physiologist ; it is part of his mission, not to explain illusions, but to produce them. Subject only to laws established by the limitations of the eye, he is master of the domain of fancy, of that *pays bleu* of the impossible that it is his privilege to throw open to the charmed imagination.

Of the means of wall-decoration already named, fresco-painting and stucco-panelling were generally preferred by Italian decorators, and wood-panelling and tapestries by those of northern Europe. The use of arras naturally commended itself to the northern noble, shivering in his draughty castles and obliged to carry from one to another the furniture and hangings that the unsettled state of the country made it impossible to leave behind him. Italy, however, long supplied the finest designs to the tapestry-looms of northern Europe, as the Italian painters provided ready-made backgrounds of peaked hills, winding torrents and pinnacled cities to the German engravers and the Flemish painters of their day.

Tapestry, in the best periods of house-decoration, was always subordinated to the architectural lines of the room (see Plate XI). Where it was not specially woven for the panels it was intended to fill, the subdivisions of the wall-spaces were adapted to its dimensions. It was carefully fitted into the panelling of the room, and never made to turn an angle, as wall-paper does in modern rooms, nor combined with other odds and ends of decoration. If a room was tapestried, it was tapestried, not decorated in some other way, with bits of tapestry hung here and there at random over the fundamental lines of the decoration. Nothing

can be more beautiful than tapestry properly used; but hung up
without regard to the composition of the room, here turning an
angle, there covering a part of the dado or overlapping a pilaster,
it not only loses its own value, but destroys the whole scheme of
decoration with which it is thus unmeaningly combined.

Italian panelling was of stone, marble or stucco, while in northern Europe it was so generally of wood that (in England especially) the term *panelling* has become almost synonymous with
wood-panelling, and in some minds there is a curious impression
that any panelling not of wood is a sham. As a matter of fact,
wood-panelling was used in northern Europe simply because it
kept the cold out more successfully than a *revêtement* of stone or
plaster; while south of the Alps its use was avoided for the
equally good reason that in hot climates it attracts vermin.

If priority of use be held as establishing a standard in decoration, wood-panelling should be regarded as a sham and plaster-
panelling as its lawful prototype; for the use of stucco in the
panelling of walls and ceilings is highly characteristic of Roman
interior decoration, and wood-panelling as at present used is certainly of later origin. But nothing can be more idle than such
comparisons, nor more misleading than the idea that stucco is a
sham because it seeks to imitate wood. It does not seek to imitate wood. It is a recognized substance, of incalculable value for
decorative effect, and no more owes its place in decoration to
a fancied resemblance to some other material than the nave of a
cathedral owes its place in architecture to the fancied resemblance
to a ship.

In the hands of a great race of artistic *virtuosi* like the Italians,
stucco has produced effects of beauty which in any other substance would have lost something of their freshness, their plastic

spontaneity. From the delicate traceries of the Roman baths and the loveliness of Agostino da Duccio's chapel-front at Perugia, to the improvised bravura treatment of the Farnese theatre at Parma, it has served, through every phase of Italian art, to embody the most refined and studied, as well as the most audacious and ephemeral, of decorative conceptions.

It must not be supposed that because painting, panelling and tapestry are the noblest forms of wall-decoration, they are necessarily the most unattainable. Good tapestry is, of course, very expensive, and even that which is only mediocre is beyond the reach of the average purchaser; while stuff hangings and wall-papers, its modern successors, have less to recommend them than other forms of wall-decoration. With painting and panelling the case is different. When painted walls were in fashion, there existed, below the great creative artists, schools of decorative designers skilled in the art of fresco-decoration, from the simplest kind to the most ornate. The demand for such decoration would now call forth the same order of talent, and many artists who are wasting their energies on the production of indifferent landscapes and unsuccessful portraits might, in the quite different field of decorative painting, find the true expression of their talent.

To many minds the mention of a frescoed room suggests the image of a grandiose saloon, with gods and goddesses of heroic size crowding the domed ceiling and lofty walls; but the heroic style of fresco-painting is only one of its many phases. To see how well this form of decoration may be adapted to small modern rooms and to our present way of living, it is only necessary to study the walls of the little Pompeian houses, with their delicate arabesques and slender, fanciful figures, or to note the manner in which the Italian painters treated the small rooms of the casino or garden-pavilion which formed part of every Italian country-seat. Examples of this light style of decoration may be found in the Casino del grotto in the grounds of the Palazzo del T at Mantua, in some of the smaller rooms of the hunting-lodge of Stupinigi near Turin, and in the casino of the Villa Valmarana near Vicenza, where the frescoes are by Tiepolo; while in France a pleasing instance of the same style of treatment is seen in the small octagonal pavilion called the Belvédère, frescoed by Le Riche, in the gardens of the Petit Trianon at Versailles.

As regards panelling, it has already been said that if the effect produced be satisfactory to the eye, the substance used is a matter of indifference.   Stone-panelling has the merit of solidity, and the outlines of massive stone mouldings are strong and dignified; but the same effect may be produced in stucco, a material as well suited to the purpose as stone, save for its greater fragility. Wood-panelling is adapted to the most delicate carving, greater sharpness of edge and clearness of undercutting being obtainable than in stucco: though this qualification applies only to the moulded stucco ornaments used from economy, not to those modelled by hand.   Used in the latter way, stucco may be made to produce the same effects as carved wood, and for delicacy of modelling in low relief it is superior to any other material.   There is, in short, little to choose between the different substances, except in so far as one or the other may commend itself to the artist as more peculiarly suited to the special requirements of his design, or to the practical conditions regulating his work.

It is to this regard for practical conditions, and not to any fancied superiority over other materials, that the use of wood-panelling in northern Europe may most reasonably be attributed. Not only was wood easy to obtain, but it had the additional

XIII   DRAWING-ROOM AT EASTON NESTON, ENGLAND

BUILT BY NICHOLAS HAWKESMOOR, 1702

(EXAMPLE OF STUCCO DECORATION)

National Monuments Record

XIV DOORWAY WITH MARBLE ARCHITRAVE

DUCAL PALACE, MANTUA. XVI CENTURY

Alinari-Art Reference Bureau

merit of keeping out the cold: two qualities sufficient to recommend it to the common sense of French and English architects. From the decorative point of view it has, when unpainted, one undeniable advantage over stucco—that is, beauty of color and veining. As a background for the dull gilding of old picture-frames, or as a setting for tapestry, nothing can surpass the soft rich tones of oak or walnut panelling, undefaced by the application of a shiny varnish.

With the introduction of the orders into domestic architecture and the treatment of interior walls with dado and cornice, the panelling of the wall-space between those two members began to assume definite proportions. In England and France, before that time, wall-panels were often divided into small equal-sized rectangles which, from lack of any central motive, produced a most inadequate impression. Frequently, too, in the houses of the Renaissance the panelling, instead of being carried up to the ceiling, was terminated two or three feet below it— a form of treatment that reduced the height of the room and broke the connection between walls and ceiling. This awkward device of stunted panelling, or, as it might be called, of an unduly heightened dado, has been revived by modern decorators; and it is not unusual to see the walls of a room treated, as regards their base-board and cornice, as part of an order, and then panelled up to within a foot or two of the cornice, without apparent regard to the true *raison d'être* of the dado (see Plate XII).

If, then, the design of the wall-panelling is good, it matters little whether stone, stucco, or wood be used. In all three it is possible to obtain effects ranging from the grandeur of the great loggia of the Villa Madama to the simplicity of any wood-panelled parlor in a New England country-house, and from the greatest costliness to an outlay little larger than that required for the purchase of a good wall-paper.

It was well for the future of house-decoration when medical science declared itself against the use of wall-papers. These hangings have, in fact, little to recommend them. Besides being objectionable on sanitary grounds, they are inferior as a wall-decoration to any form of treatment, however simple, that maintains, instead of effacing, the architectural lines of a room. It was the use of wall-paper that led to the obliteration of the over-door and over-mantel, and to the gradual submerging under a flood of pattern of all the main lines of the wall-spaces. Its merits are that it is cheap, easy to put on and easy to remove. On the other hand, it is readily damaged, soon fades, and cannot be cleaned ; while from the decorative point of view there can be no comparison between the flat meanderings of wall-paper pattern and the strong architectural lines of any scheme of panelling, however simple. Sometimes, of course, the use of wall-paper is a matter of convenience, since it saves both time and trouble; but a papered room can never, decoratively or otherwise, be as satisfactory as one in which the walls are treated in some other manner.

The hanging of walls with chintz or any other material is even more objectionable than the use of wall-paper, since it has not the saving merit of cheapness. The custom is probably a survival of the time when wall-decorations had to be made in movable shape; and this facility of removal points to the one good reason for using stuff hangings. In a hired house, if the wall-decorations are ugly, and it is necessary to hide them, the rooms may be hung with stuff which the departing tenant can take away. In other words, stuff hangings are serviceable if used as a tent;

as a permanent mode of decoration they are both unhealthy and inappropriate. There is something unpleasant in the idea of a dust-collecting fabric fixed to the wall, so that it cannot be shaken out at will like a curtain. Textile fabrics are meant to be moved, folded, shaken: they have none of the qualities of permanence and solidity which we associate with the walls of a room. The much-derided marble curtains of the Jesuit church in Venice are no more illogical than stuff wall-hangings.

In decorating the walls of a room, the first point to be considered is whether they are to form a background for its contents, or to be in themselves its chief decoration. In many cases the disappointing effects of wall-decoration are due to the fact that this important distinction has been overlooked. In rooms that are to be hung with prints or pictures, the panelling or other treatment of the walls should be carefully designed with a view to the size and number of the pictures. Pictures should never be hung against a background of pattern. Nothing is more distressing than the sight of a large oil-painting in a ponderous frame seemingly suspended from a spray of wild roses or any of the other naturalistic vegetation of the modern wall-paper. The overlaying of pattern is always a mistake. It produces a confusion of line in which the finest forms lose their individuality and significance.

It is also important to avoid hanging pictures or prints too close to each other. Not only do the colors clash, but the different designs of the frames, some of which may be heavy, with deeply recessed mouldings, while others are flat and carved in low relief, produce an equally discordant impression. Every one recognizes the necessity of selecting the mouldings and other ornamental details of a room with a view to their position in the scheme of decoration; but few stop to consider that in a room hung with pictures, the frames take the place of wall-mouldings, and consequently must be chosen and placed as though they were part of a definite decorative composition.

Pictures and prints should be fastened to the wall, not hung by a cord or wire, nor allowed to tilt forward at an angle. The latter arrangement is specially disturbing since it throws the picture-frames out of the line of the wall. It must never be forgotten that pictures on a wall, whether set in panels or merely framed and hung, inevitably become a part of the wall-decoration. In the seventeenth and eighteenth centuries, in rooms of any importance, pictures were always treated as a part of the decoration, and frequently as panels sunk in the wall in a setting of carved wood or stucco mouldings (see paintings in Plates V and XIX). Even when not set in panels, they were always fixed to the wall, and their frames, whether of wood or stucco, were made to correspond with the ornamental detail of the rest of the room. Beautiful examples of this mode of treatment are seen in many English interiors of the seventeenth and eighteenth centuries,[1] and some of the finest carvings of Grinling Gibbons were designed for this purpose.

Even where the walls are not to be hung with pictures, it is necessary to consider what kind of background the furniture and objects of art require. If the room is to be crowded with cabinets, bookcases and other tall pieces, and these, as well as the tables and mantel-shelf, are to be covered with porcelain vases, bronze statuettes, ivories, Chinese monsters and Chelsea groups, a plain background should be provided for this many-colored medley. Should the room contain only a few important pieces

1 See the saloon at Easton Neston, built by Nicholas Hawkesmoor (Plate XIII), and various examples given in Pyne's *Royal Residences*.

of furniture, and one or two vases or busts, the walls against which these strongly marked objects are to be placed may receive a more decorative treatment. It is only in rooms used for entertaining, dining, or some special purpose for which little furniture is required, that the walls should receive a more elaborate scheme of decoration.

Where the walls are treated in an architectural manner, with a well-designed dado and cornice, and an over-mantel and over-doors connecting the openings with the cornice, it will be found that in a room of average size the intervening wall-spaces may be tinted in a uniform color and left unornamented. If the fundamental lines are right, very little decorative detail is needed to complete the effect; whereas, when the lines are wrong, no overlaying of ornamental odds and ends, in the way of pictures, bric-à-brac and other improvised expedients, will conceal the structural deficiencies.

IV

DOORS

THE fate of the door in America has been a curious one, and had the other chief features of the house — such as windows, fireplaces, and stairs — been pursued with the same relentless animosity by architects and decorators, we should no longer be living in houses at all. First, the door was slid into the wall; then even its concealed presence was resented, and it was unhung and replaced by a portière; while of late it has actually ceased to form a part of house-building, and many recently built houses contain doorways *without doors*. Even the front door, which might seem to have too valid a reason for existence to be disturbed by the variations of fashion, has lately had to yield its place, in the more pretentious kind of house, to a wrought-iron gateway lined with plate-glass, against which, as a climax of inconsequence, a thick curtain is usually hung.

It is not difficult to explain such architectural vagaries. In general, their origin is to be found in the misapplication of some serviceable feature and its consequent rejection by those who did not understand that it had ceased to be useful only because it was not properly used.

In the matter of doors, such an explanation at once presents itself. During the latter half of the eighteenth century it occurred to some ingenious person that when two adjoining rooms were used for entertaining, and it was necessary to open the doors between them, these doors might be in the way; and to avoid this possibility, a recess was formed in the thickness of the wall, and the door was made to slide into it.

This idea apparently originated in England, for sliding doors, even in the present day, are virtually unknown on the continent; and Isaac Ware, in the book already quoted, speaks of the sliding door as having been used "at the house, late Mr. de Pestre's, near Hanover Square," and adds that "the manner of it there may serve as an example to other builders," showing it to have been a novelty which he thought worthy of imitation.

English taste has never been so sure as that of the Latin races; and it has, moreover, been perpetually modified by a passion for contriving all kinds of supposed "conveniences," which instead of simplifying life not unfrequently tend to complicate it. Americans have inherited this trait, and in both countries the architect or upholsterer who can present a new and more intricate way of planning a house or of making a piece of furniture, is more sure of a hearing than he who follows the accepted lines.

It is doubtful if the devices to which so much is sacrificed in English and American house-planning always offer the practical advantages attributed to them. In the case of the sliding door these advantages are certainly open to question, since there is no reason why a door should not open into a room. Under ordinary circumstances, doors should always be kept shut; it is only, as Ware points out, when two adjoining rooms are used for entertaining that it is necessary to leave the door between them open. Now, between two rooms destined for entertaining, a double door (*à deux battants*) is always preferable to a single one; and as an

opening four feet six inches wide is sufficient in such cases, each
of the doors will be only two feet three inches wide, and therefore
cannot encroach to any serious extent on the floor-space of the
room.   On the other hand, much has been sacrificed to the
supposed "convenience" of the sliding door: first, the decorative
effect of a well-panelled door, with hinges, box-locks and handle
of finely chiselled bronze ; secondly, the privacy of both rooms,
since the difficulty of closing a heavy sliding door always leads to
its being left open, with the result that two rooms are necessarily
used as one.   In fact, the absence of privacy in modern houses
is doubtless in part due to the difficulty of closing the doors between the rooms.

The sliding door has led to another abuse in house-planning :
the exaggerated widening of the doorway.   While doors were
hung on hinges, doorways were of necessity restricted to their
proper dimensions; but with the introduction of the sliding door,
openings eight or ten feet wide became possible.   The planning
of a house is often modified by a vague idea on the part of its
owners that they may wish to give entertainments on a large
scale.   As a matter of fact, general entertainments are seldom
given in a house of average size; and those who plan their houses
with a view to such possibilities sacrifice their daily comfort to
an event occurring perhaps once a year.   But even where many
entertainments are to be given large doorways are of little use.
Any architect of experience knows that ease of circulation depends far more on the planning of the house and on the position
of the openings than on the actual dimensions of the latter.
Indeed, two moderate-sized doorways leading from one room
to another are of much more use in facilitating the movements
of a crowd than one opening ten feet wide.

Sliding doors have been recommended on the ground that their use preserves a greater amount of wall-space; but two doorways of moderate dimensions, properly placed, will preserve as much wall-space as one very large opening and will probably permit a better distribution of panelling and furniture. There was far more wall-space in seventeenth and eighteenth-century rooms than there is in rooms of the same dimensions in the average modern American house; and even where this space was not greater in actual measurement, more furniture could be used, since the openings were always placed with a view to the proper arrangement of what the room was to contain.

According to the best authorities, the height of a well-proportioned doorway should be twice its width; and as the height is necessarily regulated by the stud of the room, it follows that the width varies; but it is obvious that no doorway should be less than six feet high nor less than three feet wide.

When a doorway is over three feet six inches wide, a pair of doors should always be used; while a single door is preferable in a narrow opening.

In rooms twelve feet or less in height, doorways should not be more than nine feet high. The width of openings in such rooms is therefore restricted to four feet six inches; indeed, it is permissible to make the opening lower and thus reduce its width to four feet; six inches of additional wall-space are not to be despised in a room of average dimensions.

The treatment of the door forms one of the most interesting chapters in the history of house-decoration. In feudal castles the interior doorway, for purposes of defense, was made so small and narrow that only one person could pass through at a time, and was set in a plain lintel or architrave of stone, the door itself being fortified by bands of steel or iron, and by heavy bolts and bars. Even at this early period it seems probable that in the chief apartments the lines of the doorway were carried up to the ceiling by means of an over-door of carved wood, or of some painted decorative composition.[1] This connection between the doorway and the ceiling, maintained through all the subsequent phases of house-decoration, was in fact never disregarded until the beginning of the present century.

It was in Italy that the door, in common with the other features of private dwellings, first received a distinctly architectural treatment. In Italian palaces of the fifteenth century the doorways were usually framed by architraves of marble, enriched with arabesques, medallions and processional friezes in low relief, combined with disks of colored marble. Interesting examples of this treatment are seen in the apartments of Isabella of Este in the ducal palace at Mantua (see Plate XIV), in the ducal palace at Urbino, and in the Certosa of Pavia — some of the smaller doorways in this monastery being decorated with medallion portraits of the Sforzas, and with other low reliefs of extraordinary beauty.

The doors in Italian palaces were usually of inlaid wood, elaborate in composition and affording in many cases beautiful instances of that sense of material limitation that preserves one art from infringing upon another. The intarsia doors of the palace at Urbino are among the most famous examples of this form of decoration. It should be noted that many of the woods used in Italian marquetry were of a light shade, so that the blending of colors in Renaissance doors produces a sunny golden-brown tint in perfect harmony with the marble architrave of the

[1] See Viollet-le-Duc, *Dictionnaire raisonné de l'Architecture française,* under *Porte.*

doorway. The Italian decorator would never have permitted so harsh a contrast as that between the white trim and the mahogany doors of English eighteenth-century houses. This juxtaposition of colors was disapproved by French decorators also, and was seldom seen except in England and in the American houses built under English influence. It should be observed, too, that the polish given to hard-grained wood in England, and imitated in the wood-varnish of the present day, was never in favor in Italy and France. Shiny surfaces were always disliked by the best decorators.

The classic revival in Italy necessarily modified the treatment of the doorway. Flat arabesques and delicately chiselled medallions gave way to a plain architrave, frequently masked by an order; while the over-door took the form of a pediment, or, in the absence of shafts, of a cornice or entablature resting on brackets. The use of a pediment over interior doorways was characteristic of Italian decoration.

In studying Italian interiors of this period from photographs or modern prints, or even in visiting the partly dilapidated palaces themselves, it may at first appear that the lines of the doorway were not always carried up to the cornice. Several causes have combined to produce this impression. In the first place, the architectural treatment of the over-door was frequently painted on the wall, and has consequently disappeared with the rest of the wall-decoration (see Plate XV). Then, again, Italian rooms were often painted with landscapes and out-of-door architectural effects, and when this was done the doorways were combined with these architectural compositions, and were not treated as part of the room, but as part of what the room *pretended to be*. In the suppressed Scuola della Carità (now the Academy of Fine

Arts) at Venice, one may see a famous example of this treatment in the doorway under the stairs leading up to the temple, in Titian's great painting of the "Presentation of the Virgin."[1] Again, in the high-studded Italian saloons containing a musician's gallery, or a clerestory, a cornice was frequently carried around the walls at suitable height above the lower range of openings, and the decorative treatment above the doors, windows and fireplace extended only to this cornice, not to the actual ceiling of the room.

Thus it will be seen that the relation between the openings and cornice in Italian decoration was in reality always maintained except where the decorator chose to regard them as forming a part, not of the room, but of some other architectural composition.

In the sixteenth century the excessive use of marquetry was abandoned, doors being panelled, and either left undecorated or painted with those light animated combinations of figure and arabesque which Raphael borrowed from the Roman fresco-painters, and which since his day have been peculiarly characteristic of Italian decorative painting.[2]

Wood-carving in Italy was little used in house-decoration, and, as a rule, the panelling of doors was severely architectural in character, with little of the delicate ornamentation marking the French work of the seventeenth and eighteenth centuries.[3]

In France the application of the orders to interior doorways was never very popular, though it figures in French architectural

[1] This painting has now been restored to its proper position in the Scuola della Carità, and the door which had been *painted in* under the stairs has been removed to make way for the actual doorway around which the picture was originally painted.

[2] See the doors of the Sala dello Zodiaco in the ducal palace at Mantua (Plate XVI).

[3] Some rooms of the rocaille period, however, contain doors as elaborately carved as those seen in France (see the doors in the royal palace at Genoa, Plate XXXIV).

XV   SALA DEI CAVALLI

PALAZZO DEL TE, MANTUA. XVI CENTURY

(EXAMPLE OF PAINTED ARCHITECTURAL DECORATION)

John Barrington Bayley

XVI   DOOR IN THE SALA DELLO ZODIACO

DUCAL PALACE, MANTUA. XVIII CENTURY

John Barrington Bayley

works of the eighteenth century. The architrave, except in houses of great magnificence, was usually of wood, sometimes very richly carved. It was often surmounted by an entablature with a cornice resting on carved brackets; while the panel between this and the ceiling-cornice was occupied by an over-door consisting either of a painting, of a carved panel or of a stucco or marble bas-relief. These over-doors usually corresponded with the design of the over-mantel.

Great taste and skill were displayed in the decoration of door-panels and embrasure. In the earlier part of the seventeenth century, doors and embrasures were usually painted, and nothing in the way of decorative painting can exceed in beauty and fitness the French compositions of this period.[1]

During the reign of Louis XIV, doors were either carved or painted, and their treatment ranged from the most elaborate decoration to the simplest panelling set in a plain wooden architrave. In some French doors of this period painting and carving were admirably combined; and they were further ornamented by the chiselled locks and hinges for which French locksmiths were famous. So important a part did these locks and hinges play in French decoration that Lebrun himself is said to have designed those in the Galerie d'Apollon, in the Louvre, when he composed the decoration of the room. Even in the simplest private houses, where chiselled bronze was too expensive a luxury, and wrought-iron locks and hinges, with plain knobs of brass or iron, were used instead, such attention was paid to both design and execution that it is almost impossible to find in France an old lock or hinge, however plain, that is not well designed and well made (see Plate XVII). The miserable commercial article that disgraces

[1] See the doors at Vaux-le-Vicomte and in the Palais de Justice at Rennes.

our modern doors would not have been tolerated in the most un-pretentious dwelling.

The mortise-lock now in use in England and America first made its appearance toward the end of the eighteenth century in England, where it displaced the brass or iron box-lock; but on the Continent it has never been adopted. It is a poor substitute for the box-lock, since it not only weakens but disfigures the door, while a well-designed box-lock is both substantial and ornamental (see Plate XVII).

In many minds the Louis XV period is associated with a general waviness of line and excess of carving. It has already been pointed out that even when the rocaille manner was at its height the main lines of a room were seldom allowed to follow the ca-pricious movement of the ornamental accessories. Openings being the leading features of a room, their main lines were almost invariably respected; and while considerable play of movement was allowed in some of the accessory mouldings of the over-doors and over-mantels, the plan of the panel, in general symmetrical, was in many cases a plain rectangle.[1]

During the Louis XV period the panelling of doors was fre-quently enriched with elaborate carving; but such doors are to be found only in palaces, or in princely houses like the Hôtels de Soubise, de Rohan, or de Toulouse (see Plate XVIII). In the most magnificent apartments, moreover, plain panelled doors were as common as those adorned with carving; while in the average private hôtel, even where much ornament was lavished on the panelling of the walls, the doors were left plain.

Towards the close of this reign, when the influence of Gabriel

[1] Only in the most exaggerated German baroque were the vertical lines of the door-panels sometimes irregular.

began to simplify and restrain the ornamental details of house-decoration, the panelled door was often made without carving and was sometimes painted with attenuated arabesques and grisaille medallions, relieved against a gold ground. Gabriel gave the key-note of what is known as Louis XVI decoration, and the treatment of the door in France followed the same general lines until the end of the eighteenth century. As the classic influence became more marked, paintings in the over-door and over-mantel were replaced by low or high reliefs in stucco: and towards the end of the Louis XVI period a processional frieze in the classic manner often filled the entablature above the architrave of the door (see Plate XVI).

Doors opening upon a terrace, or leading from an antechamber into a summer-parlor, or *salon frais,* were frequently made of glass; while in gala rooms, doors so situated as to correspond with the windows of the room were sometimes made of looking-glass. In both these instances the glass was divided into small panes, with such strongly marked mouldings that there could not be a moment's doubt of the apparent, as well as the actual, solidity of the door. In good decorative art first impressions are always taken into account, and the immediate satisfaction of the eye is provided for.

In England the treatment of doorway and door followed in a general way the Italian precedent. The architrave, as a rule, was severely architectural, and in the eighteenth century the application of an order was regarded as almost essential in rooms of a certain importance. The door itself was sometimes inlaid,[1] but oftener simply panelled (see Plate XI).

[1] The inlaid doors of Houghton Hall, the seat of Sir Robert Walpole, were noted for their beauty and costliness. The price of each was £200.

In the panelling of doors, English taste, except when it closely followed Italian precedents, was not always good. The use of a pair of doors in one opening was confined to grand houses, and in the average dwelling single doors were almost invariably used, even in openings over three feet wide. The great width of some of these single doors led to a curious treatment of the panels, the door being divided by a central stile, which was sometimes beaded, as though, instead of a single door, it were really a pair held together by some invisible agency. This central stile is almost invariably seen in the doors of modern American houses.

Towards the middle of the eighteenth century the use of highly polished mahogany doors became general in England. It has already been pointed out that the juxtaposition of a dark-colored door and a white architrave was not approved by French and Italian architects. Blondel, in fact, expressly states that such contrasts are to be avoided, and that where walls are pale in tint the door should never be dark : thus in vestibules and ante-chambers panelled with Caen stone he recommends painting the doors a pale shade of gray.

In Italy, when doors were left unpainted they were usually made of walnut, a wood of which the soft, dull tone harmonizes well with almost any color, whether light or dark; while in France it would not be easy to find an unpainted door, except in rooms where the wall-panelling is also of natural wood.

In the better type of house lately built in America there is seen a tendency to return to the use of doors hung on hinges. These, however, have been so long out of favor that the rules regulating their dimensions have been lost sight of, and the modern door and architrave are seldom satisfactory in these respects. The principles of proportion have been further disturbed by a return to the confused and hesitating system of panelling prevalent in England during the Tudor and Elizabethan periods.

The old French and Italian architects never failed to respect that rule of decorative composition which prescribes that where there is any division of parts, one part shall unmistakably predominate. In conformity with this rule, the principal panel in doors of French or Italian design is so much higher than the others that these are at once seen to be merely accessory; whereas many of our modern doors are cut up into so many small panels, and the central one so little exceeds the others in height, that they do not "compose."

The architrave of the modern door has been neglected for the same reasons as the window-architrave. The use of the heavy sliding door, which could not be opened or shut without an effort, led to the adoption of the portière; and the architrave, being thus concealed, was no longer regarded as a feature of any importance in the decoration of the room.

The portière has always been used, as old prints and pictures show; but, like the curtain, in earlier days it was simply intended to keep out currents of air, and was consequently seldom seen in well-built houses, where double sets of doors served far better to protect the room from draughts. In less luxurious rooms, where there were no double doors, and portières had to be used, these were made as scant and unobtrusive as possible. The device of draping stuffs about the doorway, thus substituting a textile architrave for one of wood or stone, originated with the modern upholsterer; and it is now not unusual to see a wide opening with no door in it, enclosed in yards and yards of draperies which cannot even be lowered at will.

The portière, besides causing a break in architectural lines, has become one of the chief expenses in the decoration of the modern room; indeed, the amount spent in buying yards of plush or damask, with the addition of silk cord, tassels, gimp and fringe, often makes it necessary to slight the essential features of the room; so that an ugly mantelpiece or ceiling is preserved because the money required to replace it has been used in the purchase of portières. These superfluous draperies are, in fact, more expensive than a well-made door with hinges and box-lock of chiselled bronze.

The general use of the portière has also caused the disappearance of the over-door. The lines of the opening being hidden under a mass of drapery, the need of connecting them with the cornice was no longer felt, and one more feature of the room passed out of the architect's hands into those of the upholsterer, or, as he might more fitly be called, the house-dressmaker.

The return to better principles of design will do more than anything else to restore the architectural lines of the room. Those who use portières generally do so from an instinctive feeling that a door is an ugly thing that ought to be hidden, and modern doors are in fact ugly; but when architects give to the treatment of openings the same attention they formerly received, it will soon be seen that this ugliness is not a necessity, and portières will disappear with the return of well-designed doors.

Some general hints concerning the distribution of openings have been given in the chapter on walls. It may be noted in addition that while all doorways in a room should, as a rule, be of one height, there are cases where certain clearly subordinate openings may be lower than those which contain doors *à deux battants*. In such cases the panelling of the door must be carefully modified in accordance with the dimensions of the opening,

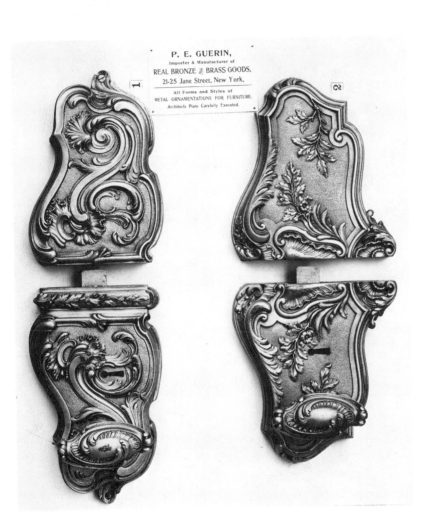

XVII EXAMPLES OF MODERN LOCKSMITH'S
WORK IN THE FRENCH STYLE

XVI OR EARLY XVII CENTURY

P. E. Guerin & Co., Inc.

XVIII CARVED DOOR

PALACE OF VERSAILLES. LOUIS XV PERIOD

(SHOWING PAINTED OVER-DOOR)

and the treatment of the over-doors in their relation to each other must be studied with equal attention. Examples of such adaptations are to be found in many old French and Italian rooms.[1]

Doors should always swing *into* a room. This facilitates entrance and gives the hospitable impression that everything is made easy to those who are coming in. Doors should furthermore be so hung that they screen that part of the room in which the occupants usually sit. In small rooms, especially those in town houses, this detail cannot be too carefully considered. The fact that so many doors open in the wrong way is another excuse for the existence of portières.

A word must also be said concerning the actual making of the door. There is a general impression that veneered doors or furniture are cheap substitutes for articles made of solid blocks of wood. As a matter of fact, owing to the high temperature of American houses, all well-made wood-work used in this country is of necessity composed of at least three, and often of five, layers of wood. This method of veneering, in which the layers are so placed that the grain runs in different directions, is the only way of counteracting the shrinking and swelling of the wood under artificial heat.

To some minds the concealed door represents one of those architectural deceptions which no necessity can excuse. It is certain that the concealed door is an expedient, and that in a well-planned house there should be no need for expedients, unless the architect is hampered by limitations of space, as is the case in designing the average American town house. Architects all know how many principles of beauty and fitness must be sacri-

[1] See a room in the Ministère de la Marine at Paris, where a subordinate door is cleverly treated in connection with one of more importance.

ficed to the restrictions of a plot of ground twenty-five feet wide by seventy-five or a hundred in length. Under such conditions, every device is permissible that helps to produce an effect of spaciousness and symmetry without interfering with convenience: chief among these contrivances being the concealed door.

Such doors are often useful in altering or adding to a badly planned house. It is sometimes desirable to give increased facilities of communication without adding to the visible number of openings in any one room; while in other cases the limited amount of wall-space may make it difficult to find place for a doorway corresponding in dimensions with the others; or, again, where it is necessary to make a closet under the stairs, the architrave of a visible door may clash awkwardly with the string-board.

Under such conditions the concealed door naturally suggests itself. To those who regard its use as an offense against artistic integrity, it must once more be pointed out that architecture addresses itself not to the moral sense, but to the eye. The existing confusion on this point is partly due to the strange analogy drawn by modern critics between artistic sincerity and moral law. Analogies are the most dangerous form of reasoning: they connect resemblances, but disguise facts; and in this instance nothing can be more fallacious than to measure the architect's action by an ethical standard.

"Sincerity," in many minds, is chiefly associated with speaking the truth; but architectural sincerity is simply obedience to certain visual requirements, one of which demands that what are at once seen to be the main lines of a room or house shall be acknowledged as such in the application of ornament. The same architectural principles demand that the main lines of a room shall not be unnecessarily interrupted; and in certain cases it would be bad taste to disturb the equilibrium of wall-spaces and decoration by introducing a visible door leading to some unimportant closet or passageway, of which the existence need not be known to any but the inmates of the house. It is in such cases that the concealed door is a useful expedient. It can hardly be necessary to point out that it would be a great mistake to place a concealed door in a main opening. These openings should always be recognized as one of the chief features of the room, and so treated by the decorator; but this point has already been so strongly insisted upon that it is reverted to here only in order to show how different are the requirements which justify concealment.

The concealed door has until recently been used so little by American architects that its construction is not well understood, and it is often hung on ordinary visible hinges, instead of being swung on a pivot. There is no reason why, with proper care, a door of this kind should not be so nicely adjusted to the wall-panelling as to be practically invisible; and to fulfil this condition is the first necessity of its construction (see concealed door in Plate XLV).

V

WINDOWS

IN the decorative treatment of a room the importance of openings can hardly be overestimated. Not only do they represent the three chief essentials of its comfort,—light, heat and means of access,—but they are the leading features in that combination of voids and masses that forms the basis of architectural harmony. In fact, it is chiefly because the decorative value of openings has ceased to be recognized that modern rooms so seldom produce a satisfactory and harmonious impression. It used to be thought that the effect of a room depended on the treatment of its wall-spaces and openings; now it is supposed to depend on its curtains and furniture. Accessory details have crowded out the main decorative features; and, as invariably happens when the relation of parts is disturbed, everything in the modern room has been thrown out of balance by this confusion between the essential and the incidental in decoration.[1]

The return to a more architectural treatment of rooms and to a recognition of the decorative value of openings, besides pro-

[1] As an example of the extent to which openings have come to be ignored as factors in the decorative composition of a room, it is curious to note that in Eastlake's well-known *Hints on Household Taste* no mention is made of doors, windows or fireplaces. Compare this point of view with that of the earlier decorators, from Vignola to Roubo and Ware.

ducing much better results, would undoubtedly reduce the expense of house-decoration. A small quantity of ornament, properly applied, will produce far more effect than ten times its amount used in the wrong way; and it will be found that when decorators rely for their effects on the treatment of openings, the rest of the room will require little ornamentation. The crowding of rooms with furniture and bric-à-brac is doubtless partly due to an unconscious desire to fill up the blanks caused by the lack of architectural composition in the treatment of the walls.

The importance of connecting the main lines of the openings with the cornice having been explained in the previous chapter, it is now necessary to study the different openings in turn, and to see in how many ways they serve to increase the dignity and beauty of their surroundings.

As light-giving is the main purpose for which windows are made, the top of the window should be as near the ceiling as the cornice will allow. Ventilation, the secondary purpose of the window, is also better served by its being so placed, since an opening a foot wide near the ceiling will do more towards airing a room than a space twice as large near the floor. In our northern States, where the dark winter days and the need of artificial heat make light and ventilation so necessary, these considerations are especially important. In Italian palaces the windows are generally lower than in more northern countries, since the greater intensity of the sunshine makes a much smaller opening sufficient; moreover, in Italy, during the summer, houses are not kept cool by letting in the air, but by shutting it out.

Windows should not exceed five feet in width, while in small rooms openings three feet wide will be found sufficient. There are practical as well as artistic reasons for observing this rule, since a sash-window containing a sheet of glass more than five feet wide cannot be so hung that it may be raised without effort; while a casement, or French window, though it may be made somewhat wider, is not easy to open if its width exceeds six feet.

The next point to consider is the distance between the bottom of the window and the floor. This must be decided by circumstances, such as the nature of the view, the existence of a balcony or veranda, or the wish to have a window-seat. The outlook must also be considered, and the window treated in one way if it looks upon the street, and in another if it gives on the garden or informal side of the house. In the country nothing is more charming than the French window opening to the floor. On the more public side of the house, unless the latter gives on an enclosed court, it is best that the windows should be placed about three feet from the floor, so that persons approaching the house may not be able to look in. Windows placed at this height should be provided with a fixed seat, or with one of the little settees with arms, but without a back, formerly used for this purpose.

Although for practical reasons it may be necessary that the same room should contain some windows opening to the floor and others raised several feet above it, the tops of all the windows should be on a level. To place them at different heights serves no useful end, and interferes with any general scheme of decoration and more specially with the arrangement of curtains.

Mullions dividing a window in the centre should be avoided whenever possible, since they are an unnecessary obstruction to the view. The chief drawback to a casement window is that its sashes join in the middle; but as this is a structural necessity, it is less objectionable. If mullions are required, they should be so placed as to divide the window into three parts, thus preserving an unobstructed central pane. The window called Palladian illustrates this point.

Now that large plate-glass windows have ceased to be a novelty, it will perhaps be recognized that the old window with subdivided panes had certain artistic and practical merits that have of late been disregarded.

Where there is a fine prospect, windows made of a single plate of glass are often preferred; but it must be remembered that the subdivisions of a sash, while obstructing the view, serve to establish a relation between the inside of the house and the landscape, making the latter what, *as seen from a room,* it logically ought to be: a part of the wall-decoration, in the sense of being subordinated to the same general lines. A large unbroken sheet of plate-glass interrupts the decorative scheme of the room, just as in verse, if the distances between the rhymes are so great that the ear cannot connect them, the continuity of sound is interrupted. Decoration must rhyme to the eye, and to do so must be subject to the limitations of the eye, as verse is subject to the limitations of the ear. Success in any art depends on a due regard for the limitations of the sense to which it appeals.

The effect of a perpetually open window, produced by a large sheet of plate-glass, while it gives a sense of coolness and the impression of being out of doors, becomes for these very reasons a disadvantage in cold weather.

It is sometimes said that the architects of the eighteenth century would have used large plates of glass in their windows had they been able to obtain them; but as such plates were frequently used for mirrors, it is evident that they were not difficult to get, and that there must have been other reasons for not employing them in windows; while the additional expense could hardly have been an obstacle in an age when princes and nobles built with such royal disregard of cost. The French, always logical in such matters, having tried the effect of plate-glass, are now returning to the old fashion of smaller panes; and in many of the new houses in Paris, where the windows at first contained large plates of glass, the latter have since been subdivided by a network of narrow mouldings applied to the glass.

As to the comparative merits of French, or casement, and sash windows, both arrangements have certain advantages. In houses built in the French or Italian style, casement windows are best adapted to the general treatment; while the sash-window is more in keeping in English houses. Perhaps the best way of deciding the question is to remember that "les fenêtres sont intimement liées aux grandes lignes de l'architecture," and to conform to the rule suggested by this axiom.

The two common objections to French windows — that they are less convenient for ventilation, and that they cannot be opened without letting in cold air near the floor — are both unfounded. All properly made French windows have at the top an impost or stationary part containing small panes, one of which is made to open, thus affording perfect ventilation without draught. Another expedient, seen in one of the rooms of Mesdames de France at Versailles, is a small pane in the main part of the window, opening on hinges of its own. (For examples of well-designed French windows, see Plates XXX and XXXI.)

Sash-windows have the disadvantage of not opening more than half-way, a serious drawback in our hot summer climate. It is often said that French windows cannot be opened wide without

XIX SALON DES MALACHITES

GRAND TRIANON, VERSAILLES. LOUIS XIV PERIOD

(SHOWING WELL-DESIGNED WINDOW WITH SOLID INSIDE SHUTTER,
AND PICTURES FORMING PART OF WALL-DECORATION)

XX   MANTELPIECE IN DUCAL PALACE, URBINO

XV CENTURY

(TRANSITION BETWEEN GOTHIC AND RENAISSANCE)

Alinari-Art Reference Bureau

interfering with the curtains; but this difficulty is easily met by the use of curtains made with cords and pulleys, in the sensible old-fashioned manner. The real purpose of the window-curtain is to regulate the amount of light admitted to the room, and a curtain so arranged that it cannot be drawn backward and forward at will is but a meaningless accessory. It was not until the beginning of the present century that curtains were used without regard to their practical purpose. The window-hangings of the middle ages and of the Renaissance were simply straight pieces of cloth or tapestry hung across the window without any attempt at drapery, and regarded not as part of the decoration of the room, but as a necessary protection against draughts. It is probably for this reason that in old prints and pictures representing the rooms of wealthy people, curtains are so seldom seen. The better the house, the less need there was for curtains. In the engravings of Abraham Bosse, which so faithfully represent the interior decoration of every class of French house during the reign of Louis XIII, it will be noticed that in the richest apartments there are no window-curtains. In all the finest rooms of the seventeenth and eighteenth centuries the inside shutters and embrasures of the windows were decorated with a care which proves that they were not meant to be concealed by curtains (see the painted embrasures of the saloon in the Villa Vertemati, Plate XLIV). The shutters in the state apartments of Fouquet's château of Vaux-le-Vicomte, near Melun, are painted on both sides with exquisite arabesques; while those in the apartments of Mesdames de France, on the ground floor of the palace of Versailles, are examples of the most beautiful carving. In fact, it would be more difficult to cite a room of any importance in which the windows were not so treated, than to go on enumerating examples of what was really a universal custom until the beginning of the present century. It is known, of course, that curtains were used in former times: prints, pictures and inventories alike prove this fact; but the care expended on the decorative treatment of windows makes it plain that the curtain, like the portière, was regarded as a necessary evil rather than as part of the general scheme of decoration. The meagreness and simplicity of the curtains in old pictures prove that they were used merely as window shades or sun-blinds. The scant straight folds pushed back from the tall windows of the Prince de Conti's salon, in Olivier's charming picture of "Le Thé à l'Anglaise chez le Prince de Conti," are as obviously utilitarian as the strip of green woollen stuff hanging against the leaded casement of the mediæval bed-chamber in Carpaccio's "Dream of St. Ursula."

Another way of hanging window-curtains in the seventeenth and eighteenth centuries was to place them inside the architrave, so that they did not conceal it. The architectural treatment of the trim, and the practice prevalent at that period of carrying the windows up to the cornice, made this a satisfactory way of arranging the curtain; but in the modern American house, where the trim is usually bad, and where there is often a dreary waste of wall-paper between the window and the ceiling, it is better to hang the curtains close under the cornice.

It was not until the eighteenth century that the window-curtain was divided in the middle; and this change was intended only to facilitate the drawing of the hangings, which, owing to the increased size of the windows, were necessarily wider and heavier. The curtain continued to hang down in straight folds, pulled back at will to permit the opening of the window, and drawn at night. Fixed window-draperies, with festoons and folds so arranged that they cannot be lowered or raised, are an invention of the modern upholsterer. Not only have these fixed draperies done away with the true purpose of the curtain, but they have made architects and decorators careless in their treatment of openings. The architrave and embrasure of a window are now regarded as of no more importance in the decorative treatment of a room than the inside of the chimney.

The modern use of the lambrequin as an ornamental finish to window-curtains is another instance of misapplied decoration. Its history is easy to trace. The mediæval bed was always enclosed in curtains hanging from a wooden framework, and the lambrequin was used as a kind of cornice to conceal it. When the use of gathered window-shades became general in Italy, the lambrequin was transferred from the bed to the window, in order to hide the clumsy bunches of folds formed by these shades when drawn up. In old prints, lambrequins over windows are almost always seen in connection with Italian shades, and this is the only logical way of using them ; though they are often of service in concealing the defects of badly-shaped windows and unarchitectural trim.

Those who criticize the architects and decorators of the past are sometimes disposed to think that they worked in a certain way because they were too ignorant to devise a better method ; whereas they were usually controlled by practical and artistic considerations which their critics are prone to disregard, not only in judging the work of the past, but in the attempt to make good its deficiencies. Thus the cabinet-makers of the Renaissance did not make straight-backed wooden chairs because they were incapable of imagining anything more comfortable, but because the former were better adapted than cushioned arm-chairs to the *déplacements* so frequent at that period. In like manner, the decorator who regarded curtains as a necessity rather than as part of the decoration of the room knew (what the modern upholsterer fails to understand) that, the beauty of a room depending chiefly on its openings, to conceal these under draperies is to hide the key of the whole decorative scheme.

The muslin window-curtain is a recent innovation. Its only purpose is to protect the interior of the room from public view: a need not felt before the use of large sheets of glass, since it is difficult to look through a subdivided sash from the outside. Under such circumstances muslin curtains are, of course, useful; but where they may be dispensed with, owing to the situation of the room or the subdivision of panes, they are no loss. Lingerie effects do not combine well with architecture, and the more architecturally a window is treated, the less it need be dressed up in ruffles. To put such curtains in a window, and then loop them back so that they form a mere frame to the pane, is to do away with their real purpose, and to substitute a textile for an architectural effect. Where muslin curtains are necessary, they should be a mere transparent screen hung against the glass. In town houses especially all outward show of richness should be avoided; the use of elaborate lace-figured curtains, besides obstructing the view, seems an attempt to protrude the luxury of the interior upon the street. It is needless to point out the futility of the second layer of muslin which, in some houses, hangs inside the sash-curtains.

The solid inside shutter, now so generally discarded, save in France, formerly served the purposes for which curtains and shades are used, and, combined with outside blinds, afforded all the protection that a window really requires (see Plate XIX).

These shutters should be made with solid panels, not with slats, their purpose being to darken the room and keep out the cold, while the light is regulated by the outside blinds. The best of these is the old-fashioned hand-made blind, with wide fixed slats, still to be seen on old New England houses and always used in France and Italy : the frail machine-made substitute now in general use has nothing to recommend it.

VI

FIREPLACES

THE fireplace was formerly always regarded as the chief feature of the room, and so treated in every well-thought-out scheme of decoration.

The practical reasons which make it important that the windows in a room should be carried up to the cornice have already been given, and it has been shown that the lines of the other openings should be extended to the same height. This applies to fireplaces as well as to doors, and, indeed, as an architectural principle concerning all kinds of openings, it has never been questioned until the present day. The hood of the vast Gothic fireplace always descended from the springing of the vaulted roof, and the monumental chimney-pieces of the Renaissance followed the same lines (see Plate XX). The importance of giving an architectural character to the chimney-piece is insisted on by Blondel, whose remark, "Je voudrais n'appliquer à une cheminée que des ornements convenables à l'architecture," is a valuable axiom for the decorator. It is a mistake to think that this treatment necessitates a large mantel-piece and a monumental style of panelling. The smallest mantel, surmounted by a picture or a mirror set in simple mouldings, may be as architectural as the great chimney-pieces at Urbino or Cheverny: all depends on the spirit of the treatment and on the proper relation of the different members used. Pajou's monument to Madame du Barry's canary-bird is far more architectural than the Albert Memorial.

When, in the middle ages, the hearth in the centre of the room was replaced by the wall-chimney, the fireplace was invariably constructed with a projecting hood of brick or stone, generally semicircular in shape, designed to carry off the smoke which in earlier times had escaped through a hole in the roof. The opening of the fireplace, at first of moderate dimensions, was gradually enlarged to an enormous size, from the erroneous idea that the larger the fire the greater would be the warmth of the room. By degrees it was discovered that the effect of the volume of heat projected into the room was counteracted by the strong draught and by the mass of cold air admitted through the huge chimney; and to obviate this difficulty iron doors were placed in the opening and kept closed when the fire was not burning (see Plate XXI). But this was only a partial remedy, and in time it was found expedient to reduce the size of both chimney and fireplace.

In Italy the strong feeling for architectural lines and the invariable exercise of common sense in construction soon caused the fireplace to be sunk into the wall, thus ridding the room of the Gothic hood, while the wall-space above the opening received a treatment of panelling, sometimes enclosed in pilasters, and usually crowned by an entablature and pediment. When the chimney was not sunk in the wall, the latter was brought forward around the opening, thus forming a flat chimney-breast to which the same style of decoration could be applied. This projection was seldom permitted in Italy, where the thickness of the walls made it easy to sink the fireplace, while an unerring feeling for form rejected the advancing chimney-breast as a needless break in the wall-sur-

face of the room.   In France, where Gothic methods of construction persisted so long after the introduction of classic ornament,
the habit of building out the chimney-breast continued until the
seventeenth century, and even a hundred years later French decorators described the plan of sinking the fireplace into the thickness
of the wall as the "Italian manner."   The thinness of modern
walls has made the projecting chimney-breast a structural necessity; but the composition of the room is improved by "furring
out" the wall on each side of the fireplace in such a way as to
conceal the projection and obviate a break in the wall-space.
Where the room is so small that every foot of space is valuable,
a niche may be formed in either angle of the chimney-breast, thus
preserving the floor-space which would be sacrificed by advancing the wall, and yet avoiding the necessity of a break in the
cornice.   The Italian plan of panelling the space between mantel
and cornice continued in favor, with various modifications, until
the beginning of the present century.   In early Italian Renaissance
over-mantels the central panel was usually filled by a bas-relief;
but in the sixteenth century this was frequently replaced by a
picture, not hung on the panelling, but forming a part of it.[1]   In
France the sculptured over-mantel followed the same general lines
of development, though the treatment, until the time of Louis
XIII, showed traces of the Gothic tendency to overload with ornament without regard to unity of design, so that the main lines of
the composition were often lost under a mass of ill-combined
detail.

[1] In Italy, where the walls were frescoed, the architectural composition over the
mantel was also frequently painted.   Examples of this are to be seen at the Villa
Vertemati, near Chiavenna, and at the Villa Giacomelli, at Maser, near Treviso.
This practice accounts for the fact that in many old architectural drawings of Italian
interiors a blank wall-space is seen over the mantel.

In Italy the early Renaissance mantels were usually of marble. French mantels of the same period were of stone; but this material was so unsuited to the elaborate sculpture then in fashion that wood was sometimes used instead. For a season richly carved wooden chimney-pieces, covered with paint and gilding, were in favor; but when the first marble mantels were brought from Italy, that sense of fitness in the use of material for which the French have always been distinguished, led them to recognize the superiority of marble, and the wooden mantel-piece was discarded: nor has it since been used in France.

With the seventeenth century, French mantel-pieces became more architectural in design and less florid in ornament, and the ponderous hood laden with pinnacles, escutcheons, fortified castles and statues of saints and warriors, was replaced by a more severe decoration.

Thackeray's gibe at Louis XIV and his age has so long been accepted by the English-speaking races as a serious estimate of the period, that few now appreciate the artistic preponderance of France in the seventeenth century. As a matter of fact, it is to the schools of art founded by Louis XIV and to his magnificent patronage of the architects and decorators trained in these schools that we owe the preservation, in northern Europe, of that sense of form and spirit of moderation which mark the great classic tradition. To disparage the work of men like Levau, Mansart, de Cotte and Lebrun, shows an insufficient understanding, not only of what they did, but of the inheritance of confused and turgid ornament from which they freed French art.[1] Whether our individual tastes incline us to the Gothic or to the classic style, it is

[1] It is to be hoped that the recently published English translation of M. Émile Bourgeois's book on Louis XIV will do much to remove this prejudice.

easy to see that a school which tried to combine the structure of the
one with the ornament of the other was likely to fall into incoherent modes of expression; and this was precisely what happened
to French domestic architecture at the end of the Renaissance
period. It has been the fashion to describe the art of the Louis
XIV period as florid and bombastic; but a comparison of the designs of Philibert de Lorme and Androuet Ducerceau with those
of such men as Levau and Robert de Cotte will show that what
the latter did was not to introduce a florid and bombastic manner,
but to discard it for what Viollet-le-Duc, who will certainly not
be suspected of undue partiality for this school of architects, calls
"une grandeur solide, sans faux ornements." No better illustration of this can be obtained than by comparing the mantel-pieces
of the respective periods.[1]   The Louis XIV mantel-pieces are much
simpler and more coherent in design.   The caryatides supporting
the entablature above the opening of the earlier mantels, and the
full-length statues flanking the central panel of the over-mantel,
are replaced by massive and severe mouldings of the kind which
the French call *mâle* (see mantels in Plates V and XXXVI).
Above the entablature there is usually a kind of attic or high concave member of marble, often fluted, and forming a ledge or shelf
just wide enough to carry the row of porcelain vases with which
it had become the fashion to adorn the mantel.   These vases, and
the bas-relief or picture occupying the central panel above, form
the chief ornament of the chimney-piece, though occasionally the
crowning member of the over-mantel is treated with a decoration
of garlands, masks, trophies or other strictly architectural orna-

[1] It is curious that those who criticize the ornateness of the Louis XIV style are
often the warmest admirers of the French Renaissance, the style of all others most re-
markable for its excessive use of ornament, exquisite in itself, but quite unrelated to
structure and independent of general design.

XXI   MANTELPIECE IN THE VILLA GIACOMELLI

AT MASER, NEAR TREVISO—NOW CALLED VILLA BARBARO.

XVI CENTURY

(SHOWING IRON DOORS IN OPENING)

John Barrington Bayley

XXII FRENCH FIRE-SCREEN

FROM THE CHÂTEAU OF ANET. LOUIS XIV PERIOD

ment, while in Italy and England the broken pediment is frequently employed. The use of a mirror over the fireplace is said to have originated with Mansart; but according to Blondel it was Robert de Cotte who brought about this innovation, thus producing an immediate change in the general scheme of composition. The French were far too logical not to see the absurdity of placing a mirror too high to be looked into; and the concave Louis XIV member, which had raised the mantel-shelf six feet from the floor, was removed[1] and the shelf placed directly over the entablature.

Somewhat later the introduction of clocks and candelabra as mantel ornaments made it necessary to widen the shelf, and this further modified the general design; while the suites of small rooms which had come into favor under the Regent led to a reduction in the size of mantel-pieces, and to the use of less massive and perhaps less architectural ornament.

In the eighteenth century, mantel-pieces in Italy and France were almost always composed of a marble or stone architrave surmounted by a shelf of the same material, while the over-mantel consisted of a mirror, framed in mouldings varying in design from the simplest style to the most ornate. This over-mantel, which was either of the exact width of the mantel-shelf or some few inches narrower, ended under the cornice, and its upper part was usually decorated in the same way as the over-doors in the room. If these contained paintings, a picture carrying out the same scheme of decoration was often placed in the upper part of the over-mantel; or the ornaments of carved wood or stucco filling the panels over the doors were repeated in the upper part of the mirror-frame.

[1] It is said to have been put at this height in order that the porcelain vases should be out of reach. See Daviler, " Cours d'Architecture."

In France, mirrors had by this time replaced pictures in the central panel of the over-mantel; but in Italian decoration of the same period oval pictures were often applied to the centre of the mirror, with delicate lines of ornament connecting the picture and mirror frames.[1]

The earliest fireplaces were lined with stone or brick, but in the sixteenth century the more practical custom of using iron fire-backs was introduced. At first this fire-back consisted of a small plaque of iron, shaped like a headstone, and fixed at the back of the fireplace, where the brick or stone was most likely to be calcined by the fire. When chimney-building became more scientific, the size of the fireplace was reduced, and the sides of the opening were brought much nearer the flame, thus making it necessary to extend the fire-back into a lining for the whole fireplace.

It was soon seen that besides resisting the heat better than any other substance, the iron lining served to radiate it into the room. The iron back consequently held its own through every subsequent change in the treatment of the fireplace; and the recent return, in England and America, to brick or stone is probably due to the fact that the modern iron lining is seldom well designed. Iron backs were adopted because they served their purpose better than any others; and as no new substance offering greater advantages has since been discovered, there is no reason for discarding them, especially as they are not only more practical but more decorative than any other lining. The old fire-backs (of which reproductions are readily obtained) were decorated with charming bas-reliefs, and their dark bosses, in the play of the firelight,

[1] Examples are to be seen in several rooms of the hunting-lodge of the kings of Savoy, at Stupinigi, near Turin.

form a more expressive background than the dead and unresponsive surface of brick or stone.

It was not uncommon in England to treat the mantel as an order crowned by its entablature. Where this was done, an intermediate space was left between mantel and over-mantel, an arrangement which somewhat weakened the architectural effect. A better plan was that of surmounting the entablature with an attic, and making the over-mantel spring directly from the latter. Fine examples of this are seen at Holkham, built by Brettingham for the Earl of Leicester about the middle of the eighteenth century.

The English fireplace was modified at the end of the seventeenth century, when coal began to replace wood. Chippendale gives many designs for beautiful basket-grates, such as were set in the large fireplaces originally intended for wood; for it was not until later that chimneys with smaller openings were specially constructed to receive the fixed grate and the hob-grate.

It was in England that the architectural treatment of the over-mantel was first abandoned. The use of a mirror framed in a panel over the fireplace had never become general in England, and toward the end of the eighteenth century the mantel-piece was frequently surmounted by a blank wall-space, on which a picture or a small round mirror was hung high above the shelf (see Plate XLVII). Examples are seen in Moreland's pictures, and in prints of simple eighteenth-century English interiors; but this treatment is seldom found in rooms of any architectural pretensions.

The early American fireplace was merely a cheap provincial copy of English models of the same period. The application of the word "Colonial" to pre-Revolutionary architecture and decoration has created a vague impression that there existed at that time an American architectural style. As a matter of fact, "Colonial" architecture is simply a modest copy of Georgian models; and "Colonial" mantel-pieces were either imported from England by those who could afford it, or were reproduced in wood from current English designs. Wooden mantels were, indeed, not unknown in England, where the use of a wooden architrave led to the practice of facing the fireplace with Dutch tiles; but wood was used, both in England and America, only from motives of cheapness, and the architrave was set back from the opening only because it was unsafe to put an inflammable material so near the fire.

After 1800 all the best American houses contained imported marble mantel-pieces. These usually consisted of an entablature resting on columns or caryatides, with a frieze in low relief representing some classic episode, or simply ornamented with bucranes and garlands. In the general decline of taste which marked the middle of the present century, these dignified and well-designed mantel-pieces were replaced by marble arches containing a fixed grate. The hideousness of this arched opening soon produced a distaste for marble mantels in the minds of a generation unacquainted with the early designs. This distaste led to a reaction in favor of wood, resulting in the displacement of the architrave and the facing of the space between architrave and opening with tiles, iron or marble.

People are beginning to see that the ugliness of the marble mantel-pieces of 1840–60 does not prove that wood is the more suitable material to employ. There is indeed something of unfitness in the use of an inflammable material surrounding a fireplace. Everything about the hearth should not only be, but *look*, fire-proof. The chief objection to wood is that its use necessitates the displacement of the architrave, thus leaving a flat intermediate space to be faced with some fire-proof material. This is an architectural fault. A door of which the architrave should be set back eighteen inches or more to admit of a facing of tiles or marble would be pronounced unarchitectural; and it is usually admitted that all classes of openings should be subject to the same general treatment.

Where the mantel-piece is of wood, the setting back of the architrave is a necessity; but, curiously enough, the practice has become so common in England and America that even where the mantel is made of marble or stone it is set back in the same way; so that it is unusual to see a modern fireplace in which the architrave defines the opening. In France, also, the use of an inner facing (called a *retrécissement*) has become common, probably because such a device makes it possible to use less fuel, while not disturbing the proportions of the mantel as related to the room.

The reaction from the bare stiff rooms of the first quarter of the present century — the era of mahogany and horsehair — resulted, some twenty years since, in a general craving for knick-knacks; and the latter soon spread from the tables to the mantel, especially in England and America, where the absence of the architectural over-mantel left a bare expanse of wall above the chimney-piece.

The use of the mantel as a bric-à-brac shelf led in time to the lengthening and widening of this shelf, and in consequence to the enlargement of the whole chimney-piece.

Mantels which in the eighteenth century would have been thought in scale with rooms of certain dimensions would now be considered too small and insignificant. The use of large mantel-pieces, besides throwing everything in the room out of scale, is a structural mistake, since the excessive projection of the mantel has a tendency to make the fire smoke; indeed, the proportions of the old mantels, far from being arbitrary, were based as much on practical as on artistic considerations. Moreover, the use of long, wide shelves has brought about the accumulation of super- fluous knick-knacks, whereas a smaller mantel, if architecturally designed, would demand only its conventional *garniture* of clock and candlesticks.

The device of concealing an ugly mantel-piece by folds of dra- pery brings an inflammable substance so close to the fire that there is a suggestion of danger even where there is no actual risk. The lines of a mantel, however bad, represent some kind of solid architrave,— a more suitable setting for an architectural opening than flimsy festoons of brocade or plush. Any one who can afford to replace an ugly chimney-piece by one of good design will find that this change does more than any other to improve the appearance of a room. Where a badly designed mantel can- not be removed, the best plan is to leave it unfurbelowed, simply placing above it a mirror or panel to connect the lines of the opening with the cornice.

The effect of a fireplace depends much upon the good taste and appropriateness of its accessories. Little attention is paid at pres- ent to the design and workmanship of these and like necessary appliances; yet if good of their kind they add more to the adorn- ment of a room than a multiplicity of useless knick-knacks.

Andirons should be of wrought-iron, bronze or ormolu. Sub- stances which require constant polishing, such as steel or brass, are unfitted to a fireplace. It is no longer easy to buy the old bronze andirons of French or Italian design, with pedestals surmounted by statuettes of nymph or faun, to which time has given the iridescence that modern bronze-workers vainly try to reproduce with varnish. These bronzes, and the old ormolu andirons, are now almost *introuvables;* but the French artisan still copies the old models with fair success (see Plates V and XXXVI). Andirons should not only harmonize with the design of the mantel but also be in scale with its dimensions. In the fireplace of a large drawing-room, boudoir andirons would look insignificant; while the monumental Renaissance fire-dogs would dwarf a small mantel and make its ornamentation trivial.

If andirons are gilt, they should be of ormolu. The cheaper kinds of gilding are neither durable nor good in tone, and plain iron is preferable to anything but bronze or fire-gilding. The design of shovel and tongs should accord with that of the andirons: in France such details are never disregarded. The shovel and tongs should be placed upright against the mantel-piece, or rest upon hooks inserted in the architrave: the brass or gilt stands now in use are seldom well designed. Fenders, being merely meant to protect the floor from sparks, should be as light and easy to handle as possible: the folding fender of wire-netting is for this reason preferable to any other, since it may be shut and put away when not in use. The low guards of solid brass in favor in England and America not only fail to protect the floor, but form a permanent barrier between the fire and those who wish to approach it; and the latter objection applies also to the massive folding fender that is too heavy to be removed.

Coal-scuttles, like andirons, should be made of bronze, ormolu or iron. The unnecessary use of substances which require constant polishing is one of the mysteries of English and American housekeeping: it is difficult to see why a housemaid should spend hours in polishing brass or steel fenders, andirons, coal-scuttles and door-knobs, when all these articles might be made of some substance that does not need daily cleaning.

Where wood is burned, no better wood-box can be found than an old carved chest, either one of the Italian *cassoni*, with their painted panels and gilded volutes, or a plain box of oak or walnut with well-designed panels and old iron hasps. The best substitute for such a chest is a plain wicker basket, without ornamentation, enamel paint or gilding. If an article of this kind is not really beautiful, it had better be as obviously utilitarian as possible in design and construction.

A separate chapter might be devoted to the fire-screen, with its carved frame and its panel of tapestry, needlework, or painted arabesques. Of all the furniture of the hearth, it is that upon which most taste and variety of invention have been spent; and any of the numerous French works on furniture and house-decoration will supply designs which the modern decorator might successfully reproduce (see Plate XXII). So large is the field from which he may select his models, that it is perhaps more to the purpose to touch upon the styles of fire-screens to be avoided: such as the colossal brass or ormolu fan, the stained-glass screen, the embroidered or painted banner suspended on a gilt rod, or the stuffed bird spread out in a broiled attitude against a plush background.

In connection with the movable fire-screen, a word may be said of the fire-boards which, until thirty or forty years ago, were used to close the opening of the fireplace in summer. These fire-boards are now associated with old-fashioned boarding-house parlors, where they are still sometimes seen, covered with a paper like that on the walls, and looking ugly enough to justify their disuse. The old fire-boards were very different: in rooms of any importance they were beautifully decorated, and in Italian interiors, where the dado was often painted, the same decoration was continued on the fire-boards. Sometimes the latter were papered; but the paper used was designed expressly for the purpose, with a decorative composition of flowers, landscapes, or the ever-amusing *chinoiseries* on which the eighteenth-century designer played such endless variations.

Whether the fireplace in summer should be closed by a board, or left open, with the logs laid on the irons, is a question for individual taste; but it is certain that if the painted fire-board were revived, it might form a very pleasing feature in the decoration of modern rooms. The only possible objection to its use is that it interferes with ventilation by closing the chimney-opening; but as fire-boards are used only at a season when all the windows are open, this drawback is hardly worth considering.

In spite of the fancied advancement in refinement and luxury of living, the development of the modern heating apparatus seems likely, especially in America, to do away with the open fire. The temperature maintained in most American houses by means of hot-air or hot-water pipes is so high that even the slight additional warmth of a wood fire would be unendurable. Still there are a few exceptions to this rule, and in some houses the healthy glow of open fires is preferred to the parching atmosphere of steam. Indeed, it might almost be said that the good taste and *savoir-vivre* of the inmates of a house may be guessed from the means used for heating it. Old pictures, old furniture and fine bindings cannot live in a furnace-baked atmosphere; and those who possess such treasures and know their value have an additional motive for keeping their houses cool and well ventilated.

No house can be properly aired in winter without the draughts produced by open fires. Fortunately, doctors are beginning to call attention to this neglected detail of sanitation; and as dry artificial heat is the main source of throat and lung diseases, it is to be hoped that the growing taste for open-air life and out-door sports will bring about a desire for better ventilation, and a dislike for air-tight stoves, gas-fires and steam-heat.

Aside from the question of health and personal comfort, nothing can be more cheerless and depressing than a room without fire on a winter day. The more torrid the room, the more abnormal is the contrast between the cold hearth and the incandescent temperature. Without a fire, the best-appointed drawing-room is as comfortless as the shut-up "best parlor" of a New England farm-house. The empty fireplace shows that the room is not really lived in and that its appearance of luxury and comfort is but a costly sham prepared for the edification of visitors.

VII

CEILINGS AND FLOORS

TO attempt even an outline of the history of ceilings in domestic architecture would exceed the scope of this book;
nor would it serve any practical purpose to trace the early forms
of vaulting and timbering which preceded the general adoption of
the modern plastered ceiling. To understand the development
of the modern ceiling, however, one must trace the two very
different influences by which it has been shaped: that of the
timber roof of the North and that of the brick or stone vault of
the Latin builders. This twofold tradition has curiously affected
the details of the modern ceiling. During the Renaissance, flat
plaster ceilings were not infrequently coffered with stucco panels
exactly reproducing the lines of timber framing; and in the Villa
Vertemati, near Chiavenna, there is a curious and interesting
ceiling of carved wood made in imitation of stucco (see Plate
XXIII); while one of the rooms in the Palais de Justice at Rennes
contains an elaborate vaulted ceiling constructed entirely of wood,
with mouldings nailed on (see Plate XXIV).

In northern countries, where the ceiling was simply the under
side of the wooden floor,[1] it was natural that its decoration

[1] In France, until the sixteenth century, the same word—*plancher*—was used
to designate both floor and ceiling.

should follow the rectangular subdivisions formed by open timber-framing. In the South, however, where the floors were generally of stone, resting on stone vaults, the structural conditions were so different that although the use of caissons based on the divisions of timber-framing was popular both in the Roman and Renaissance periods, the architect always felt himself free to treat the ceiling as a flat, undivided surface prepared for the application of ornament.

The idea that there is anything unarchitectural in this method comes from an imperfect understanding of the construction of Roman ceilings. The vault was the typical Roman ceiling, and the vault presents a smooth surface, without any structural projections to modify the ornament applied to it. The panelling of a vaulted or flat ceiling was as likely to be agreeable to the eye as a similar treatment of the walls; but the Roman coffered ceiling and its Renaissance successors were the result of a strong sense of decorative fitness rather than of any desire to adhere to structural limitations.

Examples of the timbered ceiling are, indeed, to be found in Italy as well as in France and England; and in Venice the flat wooden ceiling, panelled upon structural lines, persisted throughout the Renaissance period; but in Rome, where the classic influences were always much stronger, and where the discovery of the stucco ceilings of ancient baths and palaces produced such lasting effects upon the architecture of the early Renaissance, the decorative treatment of the stone vault was transferred to the flat or coved Renaissance ceiling without a thought of its being inapplicable or "insincere." The fear of insincerity, in the sense of concealing the anatomy of any part of a building, troubled the Renaissance architect no more than it did his Gothic predecessor,

XXIII   CARVED WOODEN CEILING

VILLA VERTEMATI.   XVI CENTURY

(SHOWING INFLUENCE OF STUCCO DECORATION)

XXIV CEILING IN THE PALAIS DE JUSTICE

RENNES. LOUIS XIV PERIOD

(WOODEN CEILING, IMITATING MASONRY VAULTING AND STUCCO

ORNAMENTATION)

who had never hesitated to stretch a "ciel" of cloth or tapestry
over the naked timbers of the mediæval ceiling. The duty of exposing structural forms — an obligation that weighs so heavily
upon the conscience of the modern architect — is of very recent
origin. Mediæval as well as Renaissance architects thought first
of adapting their buildings to the uses for which they were intended and then of decorating them in such a way as to give
pleasure to the eye; and the maintenance of that relation which
the eye exacts between main structural lines and their ornamentation was the only form of sincerity which they knew or cared
about.

If a flat ceiling rested on a well-designed cornice, or if a
vaulted or coved ceiling sprang obviously from walls capable
of supporting it, the Italian architect did not allow himself to be
hampered by any pedantic conformity to structural details. The
eye once satisfied that the ceiling had adequate support, the fit
proportioning of its decoration was considered far more important
than mere technical fidelity to the outline of floor-beams and
joists. If the Italian decorator wished to adorn a ceiling with
carved or painted panels he used the lines of the timbering to
frame his panels, because they naturally accorded with his decorative scheme; while, were a large central painting to be employed, or the ceiling to be covered with reliefs in stucco, he felt
no more hesitation in deviating from the lines of the timbering
than he would have felt in planning the pattern of a mosaic or
a marble floor without reference to the floor-beams beneath it.

In France and England it was natural that timber-construction
should long continue to regulate the design of the ceiling. The
Roman vault lined with stone caissons, or with a delicate tracery
of stucco-work, was not an ever-present precedent in northern

Europe. Tradition pointed to the open-timbered roof; and as Italy furnished numerous and brilliant examples of decorative treatment adapted to this form of ceiling, it was to be expected that both in France and England the national form should be preserved long after Italian influences had established themselves in both countries. In fact, it is interesting to note that in France, where the artistic feeling was much finer, and the sense of fitness and power of adaptation were more fully developed, than in England, the lines of the timbered ceiling persisted throughout the Renaissance and Louis XIII periods; whereas in England the Elizabethan architects, lost in the mazes of Italian detail, without a guiding perception of its proper application, abandoned the timbered ceiling, with its eminently architectural subdivisions, for a flat plaster surface over which geometrical flowers in stucco meandered in endless sinuosities, unbroken by a single moulding, and repeating themselves with the maddening persistency of wall-paper pattern. This style of ornamentation was done away with by Inigo Jones and his successors, who restored the architectural character of the ceiling, whether flat or vaulted; and thereafter panelling persisted in England until the French Revolution brought about the general downfall of taste.[1]

In France, at the beginning of the eighteenth century, the liking for *petits appartements* led to greater lightness in all kinds of decorative treatment; and the ceilings of the Louis XV period, while pleasing in detail, are open to the criticism of being somewhat weak in form. Still, they are always *compositions*, and their light traceries, though perhaps too dainty and fragile in themselves, are so disposed as to form a clearly marked design, instead of being allowed to wander in a monotonous network over

[1] For a fine example of an English stucco ceiling, see Plate XIII.

the whole surface of the ceiling, like the ubiquitous Tudor rose. Isaac Ware, trained in the principles of form which the teachings of Inigo Jones had so deeply impressed upon English architects, ridicules the "petty wildnesses" of the French style; but if the Louis XV ceiling lost for a time its architectural character, this was soon to be restored by Gabriel and his followers, while at the same period in England the forcible mouldings of Inigo Jones's school were fading into the ineffectual grace of Adam's laurel-wreaths and velaria.

In the general effect of the room, the form of the ceiling is of more importance than its decoration. In rooms of a certain size and height, a flat surface overhead looks monotonous, and the ceiling should be vaulted or coved.[1] Endless modifications of this form of treatment are to be found in the architectural treatises of the seventeenth and eighteenth centuries, as well as in the buildings of that period.

A coved ceiling greatly increases the apparent height of a low-studded room; but rooms of this kind should not be treated with an order, since the projection of the cornice below the springing of the cove will lower the walls so much as to defeat the purpose for which the cove has been used. In such rooms the cove should rise directly from the walls; and this treatment suggests the important rule that where the cove is not supported by a cornice the ceiling decoration should be of very light character. A heavy panelled ceiling should not rest on the walls without the intervention of a strongly profiled cornice. The French Louis XV decoration, with its fanciful embroidery of stucco ornament,

---

[1] The flat Venetian ceilings, such as those in the ducal palace, with their richly carved wood-work and glorious paintings, beautiful as they have been made by art, are not so fine architecturally as a domed or coved ceiling.

is well suited to coved ceilings springing directly from the walls in a room of low stud; while a ceiling divided into panels with heavy architectural mouldings, whether it be flat or vaulted, looks best when the walls are treated with a complete order.

Durand, in his lectures on architecture, in speaking of cornices lays down the following excellent rules: "Interior cornices must necessarily differ more or less from those belonging to the orders as used externally, though in rooms of reasonable height these differences need be but slight; but if the stud be low, as sometimes is inevitable, the cornice must be correspondingly narrowed, and given an excessive projection, in order to increase the apparent height of the room. Moreover, as in the interior of the house the light is much less bright than outside, the cornice should be so profiled that the juncture of the mouldings shall form not right angles, but acute angles, with spaces between the mouldings serving to detach the latter still more clearly from each other."

The choice of the substance out of which a ceiling is to be made depends somewhat upon the dimensions of the room, the height of the stud and the decoration of the walls. A heavily panelled wooden ceiling resting upon walls either frescoed or hung with stuff is likely to seem oppressive; but, as in all other kinds of decoration, the effect produced depends far more upon the form and the choice of ornamental detail than upon the material used. Wooden ceilings, however, both from the nature of the construction and the kind of ornament which may most suitably be applied to them, are of necessity rather heavy in appearance, and should therefore be used only in large and high-studded rooms the walls of which are panelled in wood.[1]

[1] For an example of a wooden ceiling which is too heavy for the wall-decoration below it, see Plate XLIV.

Stucco and fresco-painting are adapted to every variety of decoration, from the light traceries of a boudoir ceiling to the dome
of the *salon à l'Italienne;* but the design must be chosen with
strict regard to the size and height of the room and to the proposed treatment of its walls. The cornice forms the connecting
link between walls and ceiling and it is essential to the harmony
of any scheme of decoration that this important member should
be carefully designed. It is useless to lavish money on the adornment of walls and ceiling connected by an ugly cornice.

The same objections extend to the clumsy plaster mouldings
which in many houses disfigure the ceiling. To paint or gild a
ceiling of this kind only attracts attention to its ugliness. When
the expense of removing the mouldings and filling up the holes in
the plaster is considered too great, it is better to cover the bulbous
rosettes and pendentives with kalsomine than to attempt their
embellishment by means of any polychrome decoration. The cost
of removing plaster ornaments is not great, however, and a small
outlay will replace an ugly cornice by one of architectural design;
so that a little economy in buying window-hangings or chair-
coverings often makes up for the additional expense of these
changes. One need only look at the ceilings in the average
modern house to see what a thing of horror plaster may become
in the hands of an untrained "designer."

The same general principles of composition suggested for the
treatment of walls may be applied to ceiling-decoration. Thus it
is essential that where there is a division of parts, one part shall
perceptibly predominate; and this, in a ceiling, should be the
central division. The chief defect of the coffered Renaissance
ceiling is the lack of this predominating part. Great as may have
been the decorative skill expended on the treatment of beams and

panels, the coffered ceiling of equal-sized divisions seems to press down upon the spectator's head; whereas the large central panel gives an idea of height that the great ceiling-painters were quick to enhance by glimpses of cloud and sky, or some aerial effect, as in Mantegna's incomparable ceiling of the Sala degli Sposi in the ducal palace of Mantua.

Ceiling-decoration should never be a literal reproduction of wall-decoration. The different angle and greater distance at which ceilings are viewed demand a quite different treatment and it is to the disregard of this fact that most badly designed ceilings owe their origin. Even in the high days of art there was a tendency on the part of some decorators to confound the two plane surfaces of wall and ceiling, and one might cite many wall-designs which have been transferred to the ceiling without being rearranged to fit their new position. Instances of this kind have never been so general as in the present day. The reaction from the badly designed mouldings and fungoid growths that characterized the ceilings of forty years ago has led to the use of attenuated laurel-wreaths combined with other puny attributes taken from Sheraton cabinets and Adam mantel-pieces. These so-called ornaments, always somewhat lacking in character, become absolutely futile when viewed from below.

This pressed-flower ornamentation is a direct precedent to the modern ceiling covered with wall-paper. One would think that the inappropriateness of this treatment was obvious; but since it has become popular enough to warrant the manufacture of specially designed ceiling-papers, some protest should be made. The necessity for hiding cracks in the plaster is the reason most often given for papering ceilings; but the cost of mending cracks is small and a plaster ceiling lasts much longer than is generally

XXV   CEILING OF THE SALA DEGLI SPOSI

DUCAL PALACE, MANTUA

(BY ANDREA MANTEGNA, 1474)

XXVI   CEILING IN THE STYLE OF BÉRAIN

LOUIS XV PERIOD

thought. It need never be taken down unless it is actually falling; and as well-made repairs strengthen and improve the entire surface, a much-mended ceiling is stronger than one that is just beginning to crack. If the cost of repairing must be avoided, a smooth white lining-paper should be chosen in place of one of the showy and vulgar papers which serve only to attract attention.

Of all forms of ceiling adornment painting is the most beautiful. Italy, which contains the three perfect ceilings of the world — those of Mantegna in the ducal palace of Mantua (see Plate XXV), of Perugino in the Sala del Cambio at Perugia and of Araldi in the Convent of St. Paul at Parma — is the best field for the study of this branch of art. From the semi-classical vaults of the fifteenth century, with their Roman arabesques and fruit-garlands framing human figures detached as mere ornament against a background of solid color, to the massive goddesses and broad Virgilian landscapes of the Carracci and to the piled-up perspectives of Giordano's school of prestidigitators, culminating in the great Tiepolo, Italian art affords examples of every temperament applied to the solution of one of the most interesting problems in decoration.

Such ceilings as those on which Raphael and Giovanni da Udine worked together, combining painted arabesques and medallions with stucco reliefs, are admirably suited to small low-studded rooms and might well be imitated by painters incapable of higher things.

There is but one danger in adapting this decoration to modern use—that is, the temptation to sacrifice scale and general composition to the search after refinement of detail. It cannot be denied that some of the decorations of the school of Giovanni da Udine are open to this criticism. The ornamentation of the great loggia of the Villa Madama is unquestionably out of scale with the dimensions of the structure.   Much exquisite detail is lost in looking up past the great piers and the springing of the massive arches to the lace-work that adorns the vaulting.   In this case the composition is less at fault than the scale: the decorations of the semidomes at the Villa Madama, if transferred to a small mezzanin room, would be found to "compose" perfectly.   Charming examples of the use of this style in small apartments may be studied in the rooms of the Casino del Grotto, near Mantua.

The tendency of many modern decorators to sacrifice composition to detail, and to neglect the observance of proportion between ornament and structure, makes the adaptation of Renaissance stucco designs a somewhat hazardous undertaking; but the very care required to preserve the scale and to accentuate the general lines of the design affords good training in the true principles of composition.

Equally well suited to modern use are the designs in arabesque with which, in France, Bérain and his followers painted the ceilings of small rooms during the Louis XIV period (see Plate XXVI). With the opening of the eighteenth century the Bérain arabesques, animated by the touch of Watteau, Huet and J.-B. Leprince, blossomed into trellis-like designs alive with birds and monkeys, Chinese mandarins balancing umbrellas, and nymphs and shepherdesses under slender classical ruins.   Side by side with the monumental work of such artists as Lebrun and Lesueur, Coypel, Vouet and Natoire, this light style of composition was always in favor for the decoration of *petits appartements:* the most famous painters of the day did not think it beneath them to furnish designs for such purposes (see Plate XXVII).

In moderate-sized rooms which are to be decorated in a simple and inexpensive manner, a plain plaster ceiling with well-designed cornice is preferable to any device for producing showy effects at small cost. It may be laid down as a general rule in house-decoration that what must be done cheaply should be done simply. It is better to pay for the best plastering than to use a cheaper quality and then to cover the cracks with lincrusta or ceiling-paper. This is true of all such expedients: let the fundamental work be good in design and quality and the want of ornament will not be felt.

In America the return to a more substantial way of building and the tendency to discard wood for brick or stone whenever possible will doubtless lead in time to the use of brick, stone or marble floors. These floors, associated in the minds of most Americans with shivering expeditions through damp Italian palaces, are in reality perfectly suited to the dry American climate, and even the most anæmic person could hardly object to brick or marble covered by heavy rugs.

The inlaid marble floors of the Italian palaces, whether composed of square or diamond-shaped blocks, or decorated with a large design in different colors, are unsurpassed in beauty; while in high-studded rooms where there is little pattern on the walls and a small amount of furniture, elaborately designed mosaic floors with sweeping arabesques and geometrical figures are of great decorative value.

Floors of these substances have the merit of being not only more architectural in character, more solid and durable, but also easier to keep clean. This should especially commend them to the hygienically-minded American housekeeper, since floors that may be washed are better suited to our climate than those which must be covered with a nailed-down carpet.

Next in merit to brick or marble comes the parquet of oak or other hard wood; but even this looks inadequate in rooms of great architectural importance. In ball-rooms a hard-wood floor is generally regarded as a necessity; but in vestibule, staircase, dining-room or saloon, marble is superior to anything else. The design of the parquet floor should be simple and unobtrusive. The French, who brought this branch of floor-laying to perfection, would never have tolerated the crudely contrasted woods that make the modern parquet so aggressive. Like the walls of a room, the floor is a background: it should not furnish pattern, but set off whatever is placed upon it. The perspective effects dear to the modern floor-designer are the climax of extravagance. A floor should not only be, but appear to be, a perfectly level surface, without simulated bosses or concavities.

In choosing rugs and carpets the subject of design should be carefully studied. The Oriental carpet-designers have always surpassed their European rivals. The patterns of Eastern rugs are invariably well composed, with skilfully conventionalized figures in flat unshaded colors. Even the Oriental rug of the present day is well drawn; but the colors used by Eastern manufacturers since the introduction of aniline dyes are so discordant that these rugs are inferior to most modern European carpets.

In houses with deal floors, nailed-down carpets are usually considered a necessity, and the designing of such carpets has improved so much in the last ten or fifteen years that a sufficient choice of unobtrusive geometrical patterns may now be found. The composition of European carpets woven in one piece, like rugs, has never been satisfactory. Even the splendid *tapis de Savonnerie* made in France at the royal manufactory during the seventeenth and eighteenth centuries were not so true to the best principles of design as the old Oriental rugs. In Europe there was always a tendency to transfer wall or ceiling-decoration to floor-coverings. Such incongruities as architectural mouldings, highly modelled trophies and human masks appear in most of the European carpets from the time of Louis XIV to the present day; and except when copying Eastern models the European designers were subject to strange lapses from taste. There is no reason why a painter should not simulate loggia and sky on a flat plaster ceiling, since no one will try to use this sham opening as a means of exit; but the carpet-designer who puts picture-frames and human faces under foot, though he does not actually deceive, produces on the eye a momentary startling sense of obstruction. Any *trompe-l'œil* is permissible in decorative art if it gives an impression of pleasure; but the inherent sense of fitness is shocked by the act of walking upon upturned faces.

Recent carpet-designs, though usually free from such obvious incongruities, have seldom more than a negative merit. The unconventionalized flower still shows itself, and even when banished from the centre of the carpet lingers in the border which accompanies it. The vulgarity of these borders is the chief objection to using carpets of European manufacture as rugs, instead of nailing them to the floor. It is difficult to find a border that is not too wide, and of which the design is a simple conventional figure in flat unshaded colors. If used at all, a carpet with a border should always be in the form of a rug, laid in the middle of the room, and not cut to follow all the ins and outs of the floor, as such adaptation not only narrows the room but emphasizes any irregularity in its plan.

In houses with deal floors, where nailed-down carpets are used in all the rooms, a restful effect is produced by covering the whole of each story with the same carpet, the door-sills being removed so that the carpet may extend from one room to another. In small town houses, especially, this will be found much less fatiguing to the eye than the usual manner of covering the floor of each room with carpets differing in color and design.

Where several rooms are carpeted alike, the floor-covering chosen should be quite plain, or patterned with some small geometrical figure in a darker shade of the foundation color; and green, dark blue or red will be found most easy to combine with the different color-schemes of the rooms.

Pale tints should be avoided in the selection of carpets. It is better that the color-scale should ascend gradually from the dark tone of floor or carpet to the faint half-tints of the ceiling. The opposite combination—that of a pale carpet with a dark ceiling—lowers the stud and produces an impression of top-heaviness and gloom; indeed, in a room where the ceiling is overladen, a dark rich-toned carpet will do much to lighten it, whereas a pale floor-covering will bring it down, as it were, on the inmates' heads.

Stair-carpets should be of a strong full color and, if possible, without pattern. It is fatiguing to see a design meant for a horizontal surface constrained to follow the ins and outs of a flight of steps; and the use of pattern where not needed is always meaningless, and interferes with a decided color-effect where the latter might have been of special advantage to the general scheme of decoration.

XXVII CEILING IN THE CHÂTEAU OF CHANTILLY

LOUIS XV PERIOD

(EXAMPLE OF CHINOISERIE DECORATION)

Giraudon

XXVIII   ANTECHAMBER IN THE VILLA
CAMBIASO, GENOA

(BUILT BY ALESSI)

XVI CENTURY

VIII

ENTRANCE AND VESTIBULE

THE decoration of the entrance necessarily depends on the nature of the house and its situation. A country house, where visitors are few and life is simple, demands a less formal treatment than a house in a city or town; while a villa in a watering-place where there is much in common with town life has necessarily many points of resemblance to a town house.

It should be borne in mind of entrances in general that, while the main purpose of a door is to admit, its secondary purpose is to exclude. The outer door, which separates the hall or vestibule from the street, should clearly proclaim itself an effectual barrier. It should look strong enough to give a sense of security, and be so plain in design as to offer no chance of injury by weather and give no suggestion of interior decoration.

The best ornamentation for an entrance-door is simple panelling, with bold architectural mouldings and as little decorative detail as possible. The necessary ornament should be contributed by the design of locks, hinges and handles. These, like the door itself, should be strong and serviceable, with nothing finikin in their treatment, and made of a substance which does not require cleaning. For the latter reason, bronze and iron are more fitting than brass or steel.

In treating the vestibule, careful study is required to establish a harmony between the decorative elements inside and outside the house. The vestibule should form a natural and easy transition from the plain architecture of the street to the privacy of the interior (see Plate XXVIII).

No portion of the inside of the house being more exposed to the weather, great pains should be taken to avoid using in its decoration materials easily damaged by rain or dust, such as carpets or wall-paper. The decoration should at once produce the impression of being weather-proof.

Marble, stone, scagliola, or painted stucco are for this reason the best materials. If wood is used, it should be painted, as dust and dirt soon soil it, and unless its finish be water-proof it will require continual varnishing. The decorations of the vestibule should be as permanent as possible in character, in order to avoid incessant small repairs.

The floor should be of stone, marble, or tiles; even a linoleum or oil-cloth of sober pattern is preferable to a hard-wood floor in so exposed a situation. For the same reason, it is best to treat the walls with a decoration of stone or marble. In simpler houses the same effect may be produced at much less cost by dividing the wall-spaces into panels, with wooden mouldings applied directly to the plaster, the whole being painted in oil, either in one uniform tint or in varying shades of some cold sober color. This subdued color-scheme will produce an agreeable contrast with the hall or staircase, which, being a degree nearer the centre of the house, should receive a gayer and more informal treatment than the vestibule.

The vestibule usually has two doors: an outer one opening toward the street and an inner one giving into the hall; but when the outer is entirely of wood, without glass, and must therefore be left open during the day, the vestibule is usually subdivided by an inner glass door placed a few feet from the entrance. This arrangement has the merit of keeping the house warm and of affording a shelter to the servants who, during an entertainment, are usually compelled to wait outside. The French architect always provides an antechamber for this purpose.

No furniture which is easily soiled or damaged, or difficult to keep clean, is appropriate in a vestibule. In large and imposing houses marble or stone benches and tables should be used, and the ornamentation may consist of statues, vases, or busts on pedestals (see Plate XXIX). When the decoration is simpler and wooden benches are used, they should resemble those made for French gardens, with seats of one piece of wood, or of broad thick slats; while in small vestibules, benches and chairs with cane seats are appropriate.

The excellent reproductions of Robbia ware made by Cantagalli of Florence look well against painted walls; while plaster or terra-cotta bas-reliefs are less expensive and equally decorative, especially against a pale-blue or green background.

The lantern, the traditional form of fixture for lighting vestibules, is certainly the best in so exposed a situation; and though where electric light is used draughts need not be considered, the sense of fitness requires that a light in such a position should always have the semblance of being protected.

IX

HALL AND STAIRS

WHAT is technically known as the staircase (in German the *Treppenhaus*) has, in our lax modern speech, come to be designated as the hall.

In Gwilt's *Encyclopedia of Architecture* the staircase is defined as "that part or subdivision of a building containing the stairs which enable people to ascend or descend from one floor to another"; while the hall is described as follows: "The first large apartment on entering a house. . . . In magnificent edifices, where the hall is larger and loftier than usual, and is placed in the middle of the house, it is called a saloon; and a royal apartment consists of a hall, or chamber of guards, etc."

It is clear that, in the technical acceptance of the term, a hall is something quite different from a staircase; yet the two words were used interchangeably by so early a writer as Isaac Ware, who, in his *Complete Body of Architecture*, published in 1756, continually speaks of the staircase as the hall. This confusion of terms is difficult to explain, for in early times the staircase was as distinct from the hall as it continued to be in France and Italy, and, with rare exceptions, in England also, until the present century.

In glancing over the plans of the feudal dwellings of northern Europe it will be seen that, far from being based on any definite

XXIX   GALLERY OF THE EMPERORS OF THE
CASINO BORGHESE

(DECORATED BY ANTONIO ASPRUCCI)

LATE XVIII CENTURY

(INCLUDING THE RAPE OF PROSERPINE [IN CENTER OF ROOM] BY
G. L. BERNINI)

John Barrington Bayley

XXX   STAIRCASE IN THE PARODI PALACE, GENOA

XVI CENTURY

(SHOWING INTER-MURAL STAIRS AND MARBLE FLOOR)

conception, they were made up of successive accretions about the nobleman's keep. The first room to attach itself to the keep was the "hall," a kind of microcosm in which sleeping, eating, entertaining guests and administering justice succeeded each other or went on simultaneously. In the course of time various rooms, such as the parlor, the kitchen, the offices, the muniment-room and the lady's bower, were added to the primitive hall; but these were rather incidental necessities than parts of an organized scheme of planning.[1] In this agglomeration of apartments the stairs found a place where they could. Space being valuable, they were generally carried up spirally in the thickness of the wall, or in an angle-turret. Owing to enforced irregularity of plan, and perhaps to the desire to provide numerous separate means of access to the different parts of the dwelling, each castle usually contained several staircases, no one of which was more important than the others.

It was in Italy that stairs first received attention as a feature in the general composition of the house. There, from the outset, all the conditions had been different. The domestic life of the upper classes having developed from the eleventh century onward in the comparative security of the walled town, it was natural that house-planning should be less irregular,[2] and that more regard should be given to considerations of comfort and dignity. In early Italian palaces the stairs either ascended through the open cen-

---

[1] Burckhardt, in his *Geschichte der Renaissance in Italien,* justly points out that the seeming inconsequence of mediæval house-planning in northern Europe was probably due in part to the fact that the feudal castle, for purposes of defence, was generally built on an irregular site. See also Viollet-le-Duc.

[2] "Der gothische Profanbau in Italien . . . steht im vollen Gegensatz zum Norden durch die rationelle Anlage." Burckhardt, *Geschichte der Renaissance in Italien,* p. 28.

tral *cortile* to an arcaded gallery on the first floor, as in the Gondi palace and the Bargello at Florence, or were carried up in straight flights between walls.[1] This was, in fact, the usual way of building stairs in Italy until the end of the fifteenth century. These enclosed stairs usually started near the vaulted entranceway leading from the street to the *cortile*. Gradually the space at the foot of the stairs, which at first was small, increased in size and in importance of decorative treatment; while the upper landing opened into an antechamber which became the centre of the principal suite of apartments. With the development of the Palladian style, the whole staircase (provided the state apartments were not situated on the ground floor) assumed more imposing dimensions; though it was not until a much later date that the monumental staircase so often regarded as one of the chief features of the Italian Renaissance began to be built. Indeed, a detailed examination of the Italian palaces shows that even in the seventeenth and eighteenth centuries such staircases as were built by Fontana in the royal palace at Naples, by Juvara in the Palazzo Madama at Turin and by Vanvitelli at Caserta, were seen only in royal palaces. Even Morelli's staircase in the Braschi palace in Rome, magnificent as it is, hardly reaches the popular conception of the Italian state staircase — a conception probably based rather upon the great open stairs of the Genoese *cortili* than upon any actually existing staircases. It is certain that until late in the seventeenth century (as Bernini's Vatican staircase shows) intermural stairs were thought grand enough for the most splendid palaces of Italy (see Plate XXX).

The spiral staircase, soon discarded by Italian architects save as a

[1] See the stairs of the Riccardi palace in Florence, of the Piccolomini palace at Pienza and of the ducal palace at Urbino.

means of secret communication or for the use of servants, held its own in France throughout the Renaissance. Its structural difficulties afforded scope for the exercise of that marvellous, if sometimes superfluous, ingenuity which distinguished the Gothic builders. The spiral staircase in the court-yard at Blois is an example of this kind of skilful engineering and of the somewhat fatiguing use of ornament not infrequently accompanying it; while such anomalies as the elaborate out-of-door spiral staircase enclosed within the building at Chambord are still more in the nature of a *tour de force*,—something perfect in itself, but not essential to the organism of the whole.

Viollet-le-Duc, in his dictionary of architecture, under the heading *Château*, has given a sympathetic and ingenious explanation of the tenacity with which the French aristocracy clung to the obsolete complications of Gothic house-planning and structure long after frequent expeditions across the Alps had made them familiar with the simpler and more rational method of the Italian architects. It may be, as he suggests, that centuries of feudal life, with its surface of savagery and violence and its undercurrent treachery, had fostered in the nobles of northern Europe a desire for security and isolation that found expression in the intricate planning of their castles long after the advance of civilization had made these precautions unnecessary. It seems more probable, however, that the French architects of the Renaissance made the mistake of thinking that the essence of the classic styles lay in the choice and application of ornamental details. This exaggerated estimate of the importance of detail is very characteristic of an imperfect culture; and the French architects who in the fifteenth century were eagerly taking their first lessons from their contemporaries south of the Alps, had behind them nothing like the great synthetic tradition of the Italian masters. Certainly it was not until the Northern builders learned that the beauty of the old buildings was, above all, a matter of proportion, that their own style, freed from its earlier incoherencies, set out on the line of unbroken national development which it followed with such harmonious results until the end of the eighteenth century.

In Italy the staircase often gave directly upon the entranceway; in France it was always preceded by a vestibule, and the upper landing invariably led into an antechamber.

In England the relation between vestibule, hall and staircase was never so clearly established as on the Continent. The old English hall, so long the centre of feudal life, preserved its somewhat composite character after the *grand'salle* of France and Italy had been broken up into the vestibule, the guard-room and the saloon. In the grandest Tudor houses the entrance-door usually opened directly into this hall. To obtain in some measure the privacy which a vestibule would have given, the end of the hall nearest the entrance-door was often cut off by a screen that supported the musicians' gallery. The corridor formed by this screen led to the staircase, usually placed behind the hall, and the gallery opened on the first landing of the stairs. This use of the screen at one end of the hall had so strong a hold upon English habits that it was never quite abandoned. Even after French architecture and house-planning had come into fashion in the eighteenth century, a house with a vestibule remained the rarest of exceptions in England; and the relative privacy afforded by the Gothic screen was then lost by substituting for the latter an open arcade, of great decorative effect, but ineffectual in shutting off the hall from the front door.

The introduction of the Palladian style by Inigo Jones transformed the long and often narrow Tudor hall into the many-storied central saloon of the Italian villa, with galleries reached by concealed staircases, and lofty domed ceiling; but it was still called the hall, it still served as a vestibule, or means of access to the rest of the house, and, curiously enough, it usually adjoined another apartment, often of the same dimensions, called a saloon. Perhaps the best way of defining the English hall of this period is to say that it was really an Italian saloon, but that it was used as a vestibule and called a hall.

Through all these changes the staircase remained shut off from the hall, upon which it usually opened. It was very unusual, except in small middle-class houses or suburban villas, to put the stairs in the hall, or, more correctly speaking, to make the front door open into the staircase. There are, however, several larger houses in which the stairs are built in the hall. Inigo Jones, in remodelling Castle Ashby for the Earl of Northampton, followed this plan; though this is perhaps not a good instance to cite, as it may have been difficult to find place for a separate staircase. At Chevening, in Kent, built by Inigo Jones for the Earl of Sussex, the stairs are also in the hall; and the same arrangement is seen at Shobden Court, at West Wycombe, built by J. Donowell for Lord le Despencer (where the stairs are shut off by a screen) and at Hurlingham, built late in the eighteenth century by G. Byfield.

This digression has been made in order to show the origin of the modern English and American practice of placing the stairs in the hall and doing away with the vestibule. The vestibule never formed part of the English house, but the stairs were usually divided from the hall in houses of any importance; and it is difficult to see whence the modern architect has derived his idea of the combined hall and staircase. The tendency to merge into one any two apartments designed for different uses shows a retrogression in house-planning; and while it is fitting that the vestibule or hall should adjoin the staircase, there is no good reason for uniting them and there are many for keeping them apart.

The staircase in a private house is for the use of those who in-habit it; the vestibule or hall is necessarily used by persons in no way concerned with the private life of the inmates. If the stairs, the main artery of the house, be carried up through the vestibule, there is no security from intrusion. Even the plan of making the vestibule precede the staircase, though better, is not the best. In a properly planned house the vestibule should open on a hall or antechamber of moderate size, giving access to the rooms on the ground floor, and this antechamber should lead into the staircase. It is only in houses where all the living-rooms are up-stairs that the vestibule may open directly into the staircase without lessening the privacy of the house.

In Italy, where wood was little employed in domestic architec-ture, stairs were usually of stone. Marble came into general use in the grander houses when, in the seventeenth century, the stairs, instead of being carried up between walls, were often placed in an open staircase. The balustrade was usually of stone or marble, iron being much less used than in France.

In the latter country the mediæval stairs, especially in the houses of the middle class, were often built of wood; but this material was soon abandoned, and from the time of Louis XIV stairs of stone with wrought-iron rails are a distinctive feature of French domestic architecture. The use of wrought-iron in French decoration received a strong impulse from the genius of Jean Lamour, who, when King Stanislas of Poland remodelled the town of Nancy early in the reign of Louis XV, adorned its

XXXI STAIRCASE OF THE HÔTEL DE VILLE,
NANCY

LOUIS XV PERIOD

(BUILT BY HÉRÉ DE CORNY; STAIR-RAIL BY JEAN LAMOUR)

XXXII   STAIRCASE IN THE PALACE OF
FONTAINEBLEAU

LOUIS XV PERIOD

streets and public buildings with specimens of iron-work un-
matched in any other part of the world.   Since then French decorators have expended infinite talent in devising the beautiful
stair-rails and balconies which are the chief ornament of innumerable houses throughout France (see Plates XXXI and XXXII).

Stair-rails of course followed the various modifications of taste
which marked the architecture of the day.   In the seventeenth
and early eighteenth centuries they were noted for severe richness
of design.   With the development of the rocaille manner their lines
grew lighter and more fanciful, while the influence of Gabriel,
which, toward the end of the reign of Louis XV, brought about
a return to classic models, manifested itself in a simplified mode
of treatment.   At this period the outline of a classic baluster
formed a favorite motive for the iron rail.   Toward the close of
the eighteenth century the designs for these rails grew thin and
poor, with a predominance of upright iron bars divided at long
intervals by some meagre medallion or geometrical figure.   The
exuberant sprays and volutes of the rococo period and the architectural lines of the Louis XVI style were alike absent from these
later designs, which are chiefly marked by the negative merit of
inoffensiveness.

In the old French stair-rails steel was sometimes combined with
gilded iron.   The famous stair-rail of the Palais Royal, designed
by Coutant d'Ivry, is made of steel and iron, and the Duc d'Aumale
copied this combination in the stair-rail at Chantilly.   There is
little to recommend the substitution of steel for iron in such cases.
It is impossible to keep a steel stair-rail clean and free from rust,
except by painting it; and since it must be painted, iron is the
more suitable material.

In France the iron rail is usually painted black, though a

very dark blue is sometimes preferred.   Black is the better color, as it forms a stronger contrast with the staircase walls, which are presumably neutral in tint and severe in treatment.   Besides, as iron is painted, not to improve its appearance, but to prevent its rusting, the color which most resembles its own is more appropriate.   In French houses of a certain importance the iron stair-rail often had a few touches of gilding, but these were sparingly applied.

In England wooden stair-rails were in great favor during the Tudor and Elizabethan period.   These rails were marked rather by fanciful elaboration of detail than by intrinsic merit of design, and are doubtless more beautiful now that time has given them its patina, than they were when first made.

With the Palladian style came the classic balustrade of stone or marble, or sometimes, in simpler houses, of wood.   Iron rails were seldom used in England, and those to be found in some of the great London houses (as in Carlton House, Chesterfield House and Norfolk House) were probably due to the French influence which made itself felt in English domestic architecture during the eighteenth century.   This influence, however, was never more than sporadic; and until the decline of decorative art at the close of the eighteenth century, Italian rather than French taste gave the note to English decoration.

The interrelation of vestibule, hall and staircase having been explained, the subject of decorative detail must next be considered; but before turning to this, it should be mentioned that hereafter the space at the foot of the stairs, though properly a part of the staircase, will for the sake of convenience be called *the hall*, since in the present day it goes by that name in England and America.

In contrasting the vestibule with the hall, it was pointed out that the latter might be treated in a gayer and more informal manner than the former. It must be remembered, however, that as the vestibule is the introduction to the hall, so the hall is the introduction to the living-rooms of the house; and it follows that the hall must be as much more formal than the living-rooms as the vestibule is more formal than the hall. It is necessary to emphasize this because the tendency of recent English and American decoration has been to treat the hall, not as a hall, but as a living-room. Whatever superficial attractions this treatment may possess, its inappropriateness will be seen when the purpose of the hall is considered. The hall is a means of access to all the rooms on each floor; on the ground floor it usually leads to the chief living-rooms of the house as well as to the vestibule and street; in addition to this, in modern houses even of some importance it generally contains the principal stairs of the house, so that it is the centre upon which every part of the house directly or indirectly opens. This publicity is increased by the fact that the hall must be crossed by the servant who opens the front door, and by any one admitted to the house. It follows that the hall, in relation to the rooms of the house, is like a public square in relation to the private houses around it. For some reason this obvious fact has been ignored by many recent decorators, who have chosen to treat halls like rooms of the most informal character, with open fireplaces, easy-chairs for lounging and reading, tables with lamps, books and magazines, and all the appointments of a library. This disregard of the purpose of the hall, like most mistakes in household decoration, has a very natural origin. When, in the first reaction from the discomfort and formality of sixty years ago, people began, especially in England, to study the arrangement of the old Tudor and Elizabethan houses, many of these were found to contain large panelled halls opening directly upon the porch or the terrace. The mellow tones of the wood-work; the bold treatment of the stairs, shut off as they were merely by a screen; the heraldic imagery of the hooded stone chimney-piece and of the carved or stuccoed ceiling, made these halls the chief feature of the house; while the rooms opening from them were so often insufficient for the requirements of modern existence, that the life of the inmates necessarily centred in the hall. Visitors to such houses saw only the picturesqueness of the arrangement—the huge logs glowing on the hearth, the books and flowers on the old carved tables, the family portraits on the walls; and, charmed with the impression received, they ordered their architects to reproduce for them a hall which, even in the original Tudor houses, was a survival of older social conditions.

One might think that the recent return to classic forms of architecture would have done away with the Tudor hall; but, except in a few instances, this has not been the case. In fact, in the greater number of large houses, and especially of country houses, built in America since the revival of Renaissance and Palladian architecture, a large many-storied hall communicating directly with the vestibule, and containing the principal stairs of the house, has been the distinctive feature. If there were any practical advantages in this overgrown hall, it might be regarded as one of those rational modifications in plan which mark the difference between an unreasoning imitation of a past style and the intelligent application of its principles; but the Tudor hall, in its composite character as vestibule, parlor and dining-room, is only another instance of the sacrifice of convenience to archaism.

The abnormal development of the modern staircase-hall cannot be defended on the plea sometimes advanced that it is a roofed-in adaptation of the great open *cortile* of the Genoese palace, since there is no reason for adapting a plan so useless and so unsuited to our climate and way of living. The beautiful central *cortile* of the Italian palace, with its monumental open stairs, was in no sense part of a "private house" in our interpretation of the term. It was rather a thoroughfare like a public street, since the various stories of the Italian palace were used as separate houses by different branches of the family.

In most modern houses the hall, in spite of its studied resemblance to a living-room, soon reverts to its original use as a passageway; and this fact should indicate the treatment best suited to it. In rooms where people sit, and where they are consequently at leisure to look about them, delicacy of treatment and refinement of detail are suitable; but in an anteroom or a staircase only the first impression counts, and forcible simple lines, with a vigorous massing of light and shade, are essential. These conditions point to the use of severe strongly-marked panelling, niches for vases or statues, and a stair-rail detaching itself from the background in vigorous decisive lines.[1]

The furniture of the hall should consist of benches or straight-backed chairs, and marble-topped tables and consoles. If a press is used, it should be architectural in design, like the old French and Italian *armoires* painted with arabesques and architectural motives, or the English seventeenth-century presses made of some warm-toned wood like walnut and surmounted by a broken pediment with a vase or bust in the centre (see Plate XXXIII).

The walls of the staircase in large houses should be of panelled stone or marble, as in the examples given in the plates accompanying this chapter.

[1] For a fine example of a hall-niche containing a statue, see Plate XXX.

In small houses, where an expensive decoration is out of the question, a somewhat similar architectural effect may be obtained by the use of a few plain mouldings fixed to the plaster, the whole being painted in one uniform tint, or in two contrasting colors, such as white for the mouldings, and buff, gray, or pale green for the wall. To this scheme may be added plaster medallions, as suggested for the vestibule, or garlands and other architectural motives made of staff, in imitation of the stucco ornaments of the old French and Italian decorators. When such ornaments are used, they should invariably be simple and strong in design. The modern decorator is too often tempted by mere prettiness of detail to forget the general effect of his composition. In a staircase, where only the general effect is seized, prettiness does not count, and the effect produced should be strong, clear and telling.

For the same reason, a stair-carpet, if used, should be of one color, without pattern. Masses of plain color are one of the chief means of producing effect in any scheme of decoration.

When the floor of the hall is of marble or mosaic,—as, if possible, it should be,—the design, like that of the walls, should be clear and decided in outline (see Plate XXX). On the other hand, if the hall is used as an antechamber and carpeted, the carpet should be of one color, matching that on the stairs.

In many large houses the stairs are now built of stone or marble, while the floor of the landings is laid in wood, apparently owing to the idea that stone or marble floors are cold. In the tropically-heated American house not even the most sensitive person could be chilled by passing contact with a stone floor; but if it is thought to "look cold," it is better to lay a rug or a strip of carpet on the landing than to permit the proximity of two such different substances as wood and stone.

Unless the stairs are of wood, that material should never be used for the rail; nor should wooden stairs be put in a staircase of which the walls are of stone, marble, or scagliola. If the stairs are of wood, it is better to treat the walls with wood or plaster panelling. In simple staircases the best wall-decoration is a wooden dado-moulding nailed on the plaster, the dado thus formed being painted white, and the wall above it in any uniform color. Continuous pattern, such as that on paper or stuff hangings, is specially objectionable on the walls of a staircase, since it disturbs the simplicity of composition best fitted to this part of the house.

For the lighting of the hall there should be a lantern like that in the vestibule, but more elaborate in design. This mode of lighting harmonizes with the severe treatment of the walls and indicates at once that the hall is not a living-room, but a thoroughfare.[1]

If lights be required on the stairs, they should take the form of fire-gilt bronze sconces, as architectural as possible in design, without any finikin prettiness of detail. (For good examples, see the *appliques* in Plates V and XXXIV). It is almost impossible to obtain well-designed *appliques* of this kind in America; but the increasing interest shown in house-decoration will in time doubtless cause a demand for a better type of gas and electric fixtures. Meantime, unless imported sconces can be obtained, the plainest brass fixtures should be chosen in preference to the more elaborate models now to be found here.

Where the walls of a hall are hung with pictures, these should be few in number, and decorative in composition and coloring. No subject requiring thought and study is suitable in such a

[1] In large halls the tall *torchère* of marble or bronze may be used for additional lights (see Plate XXXII).

position. The mythological or architectural compositions of the Italian and French schools of the last two centuries, with their superficial graces of color and design, are for this reason well suited to the walls of halls and antechambers.

The same may be said of prints. These should not be used in a large high-studded hall; but they look well in a small entrance-way, if hung on plain-tinted walls. Here again such architectural compositions as Piranesi's, with their bold contrasts of light and shade, Marc Antonio's classic designs, or some frieze-like procession, such as Mantegna's "Triumph of Julius Cæsar," are especially appropriate; whereas the subtle detail of the German Little Masters, the symbolism of Dürer's etchings and the graces of Marillier or Moreau le Jeune would be wasted in a situation where there is small opportunity for more than a passing glance.

In most American houses, the warming of hall and stairs is so amply provided for that where there is a hall fireplace it is seldom used. In country houses, where it is sometimes necessary to have special means for heating the hall, the open fireplace is of more service; but it is not really suited to such a situation. The hearth suggests an idea of intimacy and repose that has no place in a thoroughfare like the hall; and, aside from this question of fitness, there is a practical objection to placing an open chimney-piece in a position where it is exposed to continual draughts from the front door and from the rooms giving upon the hall.

The best way of heating a hall is by means of a faience stove—not the oblong block composed of shiny white or brown tiles seen in Swiss and German *pensions*, but one of the fine old stoves of architectural design still used on the Continent for heating the vestibule and dining-room. In Europe, increased attention has of late been given to the design and coloring of these stoves; and if

XXXIII   FRENCH ARMOIRE

LOUIS XIV PERIOD

Museum of Decorative Arts, Paris

XXXIV   SALA DELLA MADDALENA

ROYAL PALACE, GENOA. XVIII CENTURY

(ITALIAN DRAWING-ROOM IN ROCAILLE STYLE)

better known here, they would form an important feature in the decoration of our halls. Admirable models may be studied in many old French and German houses and on the borders of Switzerland and Italy; while the museum at Parma contains several fine examples of the rocaille period.

X

THE DRAWING-ROOM, BOUDOIR, AND MORNING-ROOM

THE "with-drawing-room" of mediæval England, to which the lady and her maidens retired from the boisterous festivities of the hall, seems at first to have been merely a part of the bedchamber in which the lord and lady slept. In time it came to be screened off from the sleeping-room ; then, in the king's palaces, it became a separate room for the use of the queen and her damsels ; and so, in due course, reached the nobleman's castle, and established itself as a permanent part of English house-planning.

In France the evolution of the *salon* seems to have proceeded on somewhat different lines. During the middle ages and the early Renaissance period, the more public part of the nobleman's life was enacted in the hall, or *grand'salle*, while the social and domestic side of existence was transferred to the bedroom. This was soon divided into two rooms, as in England. In France, however, both these rooms contained beds ; the inner being the real sleeping-chamber, while in the outer room, which was used not only for administering justice and receiving visits of state, but for informal entertainments and the social side of family life, the bedstead represented the lord's *lit de parade*, traditionally associated with state ceremonial and feudal privileges.

The custom of having a state bedroom in which no one slept (*chambre de parade*, as it was called) was so firmly established that even in the engravings of Abraham Bosse, representing French life in the reign of Louis XIII, the fashionable apartments in which card-parties, suppers, and other entertainments are taking place, invariably contain a bed.

In large establishments the *chambre de parade* was never used as a sleeping-chamber except by visitors of distinction ; but in small houses the lady slept in the room which served as her boudoir and drawing-room.   The Renaissance, it is true, had introduced from Italy the *cabinet* opening off the lady's chamber, as in the palaces of Urbino and Mantua ; but these rooms were at first seen only in kings' palaces, and were, moreover, too small to serve any social purpose.   The *cabinet* of Catherine de' Medici at Blois is a characteristic example.

Meanwhile, the gallery had relieved the *grand'salle* of some of its numerous uses; and these two apartments seem to have satisfied all the requirements of society during the Renaissance in France.

In the seventeenth century the introduction of the two-storied Italian saloon produced a state apartment called a *salon ;* and this, towards the beginning of the eighteenth century, was divided into two smaller rooms : one, the *salon de compagnie*, remaining a part of the gala suite used exclusively for entertaining (see Plate XXXIV), while the other — the *salon de famille* — became a family apartment like the English drawing-room.

The distinction between the *salon de compagnie* and the *salon de famille* had by this time also established itself in England, where the state drawing-room retained its Italian name of *salone*, or saloon, while the living-apartment preserved, in abbreviated form, the mediæval designation of the lady's with-drawing-room.

Pains have been taken to trace as clearly as possible the mixed ancestry of the modern drawing-room, in order to show that it is the result of two distinct influences — that of the gala apartment and that of the family sitting-room. This twofold origin has curiously affected the development of the drawing-room. In houses of average size, where there are but two living-rooms — the master's library, or "den," and the lady's drawing-room, — it is obvious that the latter ought to be used as a *salon de famille*, or meeting-place for the whole family; and it is usually regarded as such in England, where common sense generally prevails in matters of material comfort and convenience, and where the drawing-room is often furnished with a simplicity which would astonish those who associate the name with white-and-gold walls and uncomfortable furniture.

In modern American houses both traditional influences are seen. Sometimes, as in England, the drawing-room is treated as a family apartment, and provided with books, lamps, easy-chairs and writing-tables. In other houses it is still considered sacred to gilding and discomfort, the best room in the house, and the convenience of all its inmates, being sacrificed to a vague feeling that no drawing-room is worthy of the name unless it is uninhabitable. This is an instance of the *salon de compagnie* having usurped the rightful place of the *salon de famille;* or rather, if the bourgeois descent of the American house be considered, it may be more truly defined as a remnant of the "best parlor" superstition.

Whatever the genealogy of the American drawing-room, it must be owned that it too often fails to fulfil its purpose as a family apartment. It is curious to note the amount of thought and money frequently spent on the one room in the house used by no one, or occupied at most for an hour after a "company" dinner.

XXXV   CONSOLE, FIRST QUARTER OF
EIGHTEENTH CENTURY

The Metropolitan Museum of Art, Gift of J. Pierpont Morgan, 1906

XXXVI SALON, PALACE OF FONTAINEBLEAU

To this drawing-room, from which the inmates of the house instinctively flee as soon as their social duties are discharged, many necessities are often sacrificed. The library, or den, where the members of the family sit, may be furnished with shabby odds and ends; but the drawing-room must have its gilt chairs covered with brocade, its *vitrines* full of modern Saxe, its guipure curtains and velvet carpet.

The *salon de compagnie* is out of place in the average house. Such a room is needed only where the dinners or other entertainments given are so large as to make it impossible to use the ordinary living-rooms of the house. In the grandest houses of Europe the gala-rooms are never thrown open except for general entertainments, or to receive guests of exalted rank, and the spectacle of a dozen people languishing after dinner in the gilded wilderness of a state saloon is practically unknown.

The purpose for which the *salon de compagnie* is used necessitates its being furnished in the same formal manner as other gala apartments. Circulation must not be impeded by a multiplicity of small pieces of furniture holding lamps or other fragile objects, while at least half of the chairs should be so light and easily moved that groups may be formed and broken up at will. The walls should be brilliantly decorated, without needless elaboration of detail, since it is unlikely that the temporary occupants of such a room will have time or inclination to study its treatment closely. The chief requisite is a gay first impression. To produce this, the wall-decoration should be light in color, and the furniture should consist of a few strongly marked pieces, such as handsome cabinets and consoles, bronze or marble statues, and vases and candelabra of imposing proportions. Almost all modern furniture is too weak in design and too finikin in detail to look well in a gala drawing-room.[1] (For examples of drawing-room furniture, see Plates VI, IX, XXXIV, and XXXV.)

Beautiful pictures or rare prints produce little effect on the walls of a gala room, just as an accumulation of small objects of art, such as enamels, ivories and miniatures, are wasted upon its tables and cabinets. Such treasures are for rooms in which people spend their days, not for those in which they assemble for an hour's entertainment.

But the *salon de compagnie,* being merely a modified form of the great Italian saloon, is a part of the gala suite, and any detailed discussion of the decorative treatment most suitable to it would result in a repetition of what is said in the chapter on Gala Rooms.

The lighting of the company drawing-room — to borrow its French designation — should be evenly diffused, without the separate centres of illumination needful in a family living-room. The proper light is that of wax candles. Nothing has done more to vulgarize interior decoration than the general use of gas and of electricity in the living-rooms of modern houses. Electric light especially, with its harsh white glare, which no expedients have as yet overcome, has taken from our drawing-rooms all air of privacy and distinction. In passageways and offices, electricity is of great service; but were it not that all "modern improvements" are thought equally applicable to every condition of life, it would be difficult to account for the adoption of a mode of lighting which makes the *salon* look like a railway-station, the dining-room like a restaurant. That such light is not needful in a drawing-room is shown by the fact that electric bulbs are usually covered by shades

[1] Much of the old furniture which appears to us unnecessarily stiff and monumental was expressly designed to be placed against the walls in rooms used for general entertainments, where smaller and more delicately made pieces would have been easily damaged, and would, moreover, have produced no effect.

of some deep color, in order that the glare may be made as inoffensive as possible.

The light in a gala apartment should be neither vivid nor concentrated : the soft, evenly diffused brightness of wax candles is best fitted to bring out those subtle modellings of light and shade to which old furniture and objects of art owe half their expressiveness.

The treatment of the *salon de compagnie* naturally differs from that of the family drawing-room: the latter is essentially a room in which people should be made comfortable. There must be a well-appointed writing-table; the chairs must be conveniently grouped about various tables, each with its lamp;—in short, the furniture should be so disposed that people are not forced to take refuge in their bedrooms for lack of fitting arrangements in the drawing-room.

The old French cabinet-makers excelled in the designing and making of furniture for the *salon de famille*. The term "French furniture" suggests to the Anglo-Saxon mind the stiff appointments of the gala room — heavy gilt consoles, straight-backed arm-chairs covered with tapestry, and monumental marble-topped tables. Admirable furniture of this kind was made in France; but in the grand style the Italian cabinet-makers competed successfully with the French; whereas the latter stood alone in the production of the simpler and more comfortable furniture adapted to the family living-room. Among those who have not studied the subject there is a general impression that eighteenth-century furniture, however beautiful in design and execution, was not comfortable in the modern sense. This is owing to the fact that the popular idea of "old furniture" is based on the appointments of gala rooms in palaces: visitors to Versailles or Fontainebleau are more likely to notice the massive gilt consoles and benches in the state saloons than the simple easy-chairs and work-tables of the *petits appartements*.   A visit to the Garde Meuble or to the Musée des Arts Décoratifs of Paris, or the inspection of any collection of French eighteenth-century furniture, will show the versatility and common sense of the old French cabinet-makers.   They produced an infinite variety of small *meubles*, in which beauty of design and workmanship were joined to simplicity and convenience.

The old arm-chair, or *bergère*, is a good example of this combination.   The modern upholsterer pads and puffs his seats as though they were to form the furniture of a lunatic's cell; and then, having expanded them to such dimensions that they cannot be moved without effort, perches their dropsical bodies on four little casters.   Any one who compares such an arm-chair to the eighteenth-century *bergère*, with its strong tapering legs, its snugly-fitting back and cushioned seat, must admit that the latter is more convenient and more beautiful (see Plates VIII and XXXVII).

The same may be said of the old French tables — from desks, card and work-tables, to the small *guéridon* just large enough to hold a book and candlestick.   All these tables were simple and practical in design: even in the Louis XV period, when more variety of outline and ornament was permitted, the strong structural lines were carefully maintained, and it is unusual to see an old table that does not stand firmly on its legs and appear capable of supporting as much weight as its size will permit (see Louis XV writing-table in Plate XLVI).

The French tables, cabinets and commodes used in the family apartments were usually of inlaid wood, with little ornamentation save the design of the marquetry — elaborate mounts of chiselled

XXXVII   ROOM IN THE PALACE OF
FONTAINEBLEAU

LOUIS XV PANELLING, LOUIS XVI FURNITURE

XXXVIII LIT DE REPOS

EARLY LOUIS XV PERIOD

The Metropolitan Museum of Art, Rogers Fund, 1922

bronze being reserved for the furniture of gala rooms (see Plate X). Old French marquetry was exquisitely delicate in color and design, while Italian inlaying of the same period, though coarser, was admirable in composition. Old Italian furniture of the seventeenth and eighteenth centuries was always either inlaid or carved and painted in gay colors: chiselled mounts are virtually unknown in Italy.

The furniture of the eighteenth century in England, while not comparable in design to the best French models, was well made and dignified; and its angularity of outline is not out of place against the somewhat cold and formal background of an Adam room.

English marquetry suffered from the poverty of ornament marking the wall-decoration of the period. There was a certain timidity about the decorative compositions of the school of Adam and Sheraton, and in their scanty repertoire the laurel-wreath, the velarium and the cornucopia reappear with tiresome frequency.

The use to which the family drawing-room is put should indicate the character of its decoration. Since it is a room in which many hours of the day are spent, and in which people are at leisure, it should contain what is best worth looking at in the way of pictures, prints, and other objects of art; while there should be nothing about its decoration so striking or eccentric as to become tiresome when continually seen. A fanciful style may be pleasing in apartments used only for stated purposes, such as the saloon or gallery; but in a living-room, decoration should be subordinate to the individual, forming merely a harmonious but unobtrusive background (see Plates XXXVI and XXXVII). Such a setting also brings out the full decorative value of all the drawing-room accessories — screens, andirons, *appliques*, and door and window-fastenings. A study of any old French interior will show how much these details contributed to the general effect of the room.

Those who really care for books are seldom content to restrict them to the library, for nothing adds more to the charm of a drawing-room than a well-designed bookcase: an expanse of beautiful bindings is as decorative as a fine tapestry.

The boudoir is, properly speaking, a part of the bedroom suite, and as such is described in the chapter on the Bedroom. Sometimes, however, a small sitting-room adjoins the family drawing-room, and this, if given up to the mistress of the house, is virtually the boudoir.

The modern boudoir is a very different apartment from its eighteenth-century prototype. Though it may preserve the delicate decorations and furniture suggested by its name, such a room is now generally used for the prosaic purpose of interviewing servants, going over accounts and similar occupations. The appointments should therefore comprise a writing-desk, with pigeon-holes, drawers, and cupboards, and a comfortable lounge, or *lit de repos*, for resting and reading.

The *lit de repos*, which, except in France, has been replaced by the clumsy upholstered lounge, was one of the most useful pieces of eighteenth-century furniture (see Plate XXXVIII). As its name implies, it is shaped somewhat like a bed, or rather like a cradle that stands on four legs instead of swinging. It is made of carved wood, sometimes upholstered, but often seated with cane (see Plate XXXIX). In the latter case it is fitted with a mattress and with a pillow-like cushion covered with some material in keeping with the hangings of the room. Sometimes the *duchesse*, or upholstered *bergère* with removable foot-rest in the shape of a

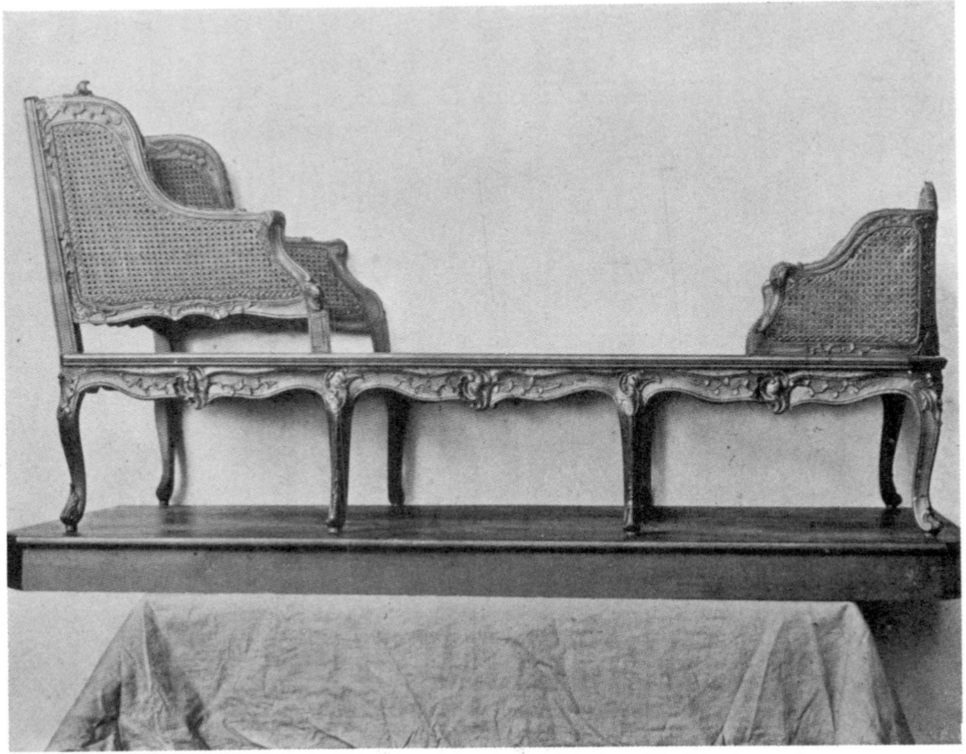

XXXIX LIT DE REPOS

LOUIS XV PERIOD

XL PAINTED WALL-PANEL AND DOOR, CHÂTEAU OF CHANTILLY

LOUIS XV

(EXAMPLE OF CHINOISERIE DECORATION)

Giraudon

square bench, is preferred to the *lit de repos;* but the latter is the more elegant and graceful, and it is strange that it should have been discarded in favor of the modern lounge, which is not only ugly, but far less comfortable.

As the boudoir is generally a small room, it is peculiarly suited to the more delicate styles of painting or stucco ornamentation described in the third chapter. A study of boudoir-decoration in the last century, especially in France, will show the admirable sense of proportion regulating the treatment of these little rooms (see Plate XL). Their adornment was naturally studied with special care by the painters and decorators of an age in which women played so important a part.

It is sometimes thought that the eighteenth-century boudoir was always decorated and furnished in a very elaborate manner. This idea originates in the fact, already pointed out, that the rooms usually seen by tourists are those in royal palaces, or in such princely houses as are thrown open to the public on account of their exceptional magnificence. The same type of boudoir is continually reproduced in books on architecture and decoration; and what is really a small private sitting-room for the lady of the house, corresponding with her husband's "den," has thus come to be regarded as one of the luxuries of a great establishment.

The prints of Eisen, Marillier, Moreau le Jeune, and other book-illustrators of the eighteenth century, show that the boudoir in the average private house was, in fact, a simple room, gay and graceful in decoration, but as a rule neither rich nor elaborate (see Plate XLI). As it usually adjoined the bedroom, it was decorated in the same manner, and even when its appointments were expensive all appearance of costliness was avoided.[1]

1 The ornate boudoir seen in many XVIIIth-century prints is that of the *femme galante.*

The boudoir is the room in which small objects of art — prints, mezzotints and *gouaches*— show to the best advantage. No detail is wasted, and all manner of delicate effects in wood-carving, marquetry, and other ornamentation, such as would be lost upon the walls and furniture of a larger room, here acquire their full value. One or two well-chosen prints hung on a background of plain color will give more pleasure than a medley of photographs, colored photogravures, and other decorations of the cotillon-favor type. Not only do mediocre ornaments become tiresome when seen day after day, but the mere crowding of furniture and gimcracks into a small room intended for work and repose will soon be found fatiguing.

Many English houses, especially in the country, contain a useful room called the "morning-room," which is well defined by Robert Kerr, in *The English Gentleman's House*, as "the drawing-room in ordinary." It is, in fact, a kind of undress drawing-room, where the family may gather informally at all hours of the day. The out-of-door life led in England makes it specially necessary to provide a sitting-room which people are not afraid to enter in muddy boots and wet clothes. Even if the drawing-room be not, as Mr. Kerr quaintly puts it, "preserved"— that is, used exclusively for company — it is still likely to contain the best furniture in the house; and though that "best" is not too fine for every-day use, yet in a large family an informal, wet-weather room of this kind is almost indispensable.

No matter how elaborately the rest of the house is furnished, the appointments of the morning-room should be plain, comfortable, and capable of resisting hard usage. It is a good plan to cover the floor with a straw matting, and common sense at once suggests the furniture best suited to such a room: two or three

Sa trifte amante abandonnee
Pleure ses maux et ses plaifirs.

XLI FRENCH BOUDOIR

LOUIS XVI PERIOD

From a Print by Le Bouteux

XLII SALON À L'ITALIENNE

(FROM A PICTURE BY COYPEL)

good-sized tables with lamps, a comfortable sofa, and chairs covered with chintz, leather, or one of the bright-colored horse-hairs now manufactured in France.

XI

GALA ROOMS: BALL-ROOM, SALOON, MUSIC-ROOM, GALLERY

EUROPEAN architects have always considered it essential that those rooms which are used exclusively for entertaining — gala rooms, as they are called — should be quite separate from the family apartments, — either occupying an entire floor (the Italian *piano nobile*) or being so situated that it is not necessary to open them except for general entertainments.

In many large houses lately built in America, with ball and music rooms and a hall simulating the two-storied Italian saloon, this distinction has been disregarded, and living and gala rooms have been confounded in an agglomeration of apartments where the family, for lack of a smaller suite, sit under gilded ceilings and cut-glass chandeliers, in about as much comfort and privacy as are afforded by the public "parlors" of one of our new twenty-story hotels. This confusion of two essentially different types of room, designed for essentially different phases of life, has been caused by the fact that the architect, when called upon to build a grand house, has simply enlarged, instead of altering, the *maison bourgeoise* that has hitherto been the accepted model of the American gentleman's house; for it must not be forgotten that the modern American dwelling descends from the English mid-

134

dle-class house, not from the aristocratic country-seat or town residence. The English nobleman's town house was like the French *hôtel*, with gates, porter's lodge, and court-yard surrounded by stables and offices; and the planning of the country-seat was even more elaborate.

A glance at any collection of old English house-plans, such as Campbell's *Vitruvius Britannicus*, will show the purely middle-class ancestry of the American house, and the consequent futility of attempting, by the mere enlargement of each room, to turn it into a gentleman's seat or town residence. The kind of life which makes gala rooms necessary exacts a different method of planning; and until this is more generally understood the treatment of such rooms in American houses will never be altogether satisfactory.

Gala rooms are meant for general entertainments, never for any assemblage small or informal enough to be conveniently accommodated in the ordinary living-rooms of the house; therefore to fulfil their purpose they must be large, very high-studded, and not overcrowded with furniture, while the walls and ceiling — the only parts of a crowded room that can be seen — must be decorated with greater elaboration than would be pleasing or appropriate in other rooms. All these conditions unfit the gala room for any use save that for which it is designed. Nothing can be more cheerless than the state of a handful of people sitting after dinner in an immense ball-room with gilded ceiling, bare floors, and a few pieces of monumental furniture ranged round the walls; yet in any house which is simply an enlargement of the ordinary private dwelling the hostess is often compelled to use the ball-room or saloon as a drawing-room.

A gala room is never meant to be seen except when crowded: the crowd takes the place of furniture. Occupied by a small number of people, such a room looks out of proportion, stiff and empty. The hostess feels this, and tries, by setting chairs and tables askew, and introducing palms, screens and knick-knacks, to produce an effect of informality. As a result the room dwarfs the furniture, loses the air of state, and gains little in real comfort; while it becomes necessary, when a party is given, to remove the furniture and disarrange the house, thus undoing the chief *raison d'être* of such apartments.

The Italians, inheriting the grandiose traditions of the Augustan age, have always excelled in the treatment of rooms demanding the "grand manner." Their unfailing sense that house-decoration is interior architecture, and must clearly proclaim its architectural affiliations, has been of special service in this respect. It is rare in Italy to see a large room inadequately treated. Sometimes the "grand manner"—the mimic *terribilità*—may be carried too far to suit Anglo-Saxon taste—it is hard to say for what form of entertainment such a room as Giulio Romano's Sala dei Giganti in the Palazzo del T would form a pleasing or appropriate background—but apart from such occasional aberrations, the Italian decorators showed a wonderful sense of fitness in the treatment of state apartments. To small dribbles of ornament they preferred bold forcible mouldings, coarse but clear-cut free-hand ornamentation in stucco, and either a classic severity of treatment or the turbulent bravura style of the saloon of the Villa Rotonda and of Tiepolo's Cleopatra frescoes in the Palazzo Labia at Venice.

The saloon and gallery are the two gala rooms borrowed from Italy by northern Europe. The saloon has already been described in the chapter on Hall and Stairs. It was a two-storied apartment, usually with clerestory, domed ceiling, and a gallery to which access was obtained by concealed staircases (see

Plates XLII and XLIII). This gallery was often treated as an arcade or loggia, and in many old Italian prints and pictures there are representations of these saloons, with groups of gaily dressed people looking down from the gallery upon the throngs crowding the floor. The saloon was used in Italy as a ball-room or gambling-room — gaming being the chief social amusement of the eighteenth century.

In England and France the saloon was rarely two stories high, though there are some exceptions, as for example the saloon at Vaux-le-Vicomte. The cooler climate rendered a clerestory less necessary, and there was never the same passion for grandiose effects as in Italy. The saloon in northern Europe was always a stately and high-studded room, generally vaulted or domed, and often circular in plan; but it seldom reached such imposing dimensions as its Italian prototype, and when more than one story high was known by the distinctive designation of *un salon à l'italienne*.

The gallery was probably the first feature in domestic house-planning to be borrowed from Italy by northern Europe. It is seen in almost all the early Renaissance châteaux of France; and as soon as the influence of such men as John of Padua and John Shute asserted itself in England, the gallery became one of the principal apartments of the Elizabethan mansion. There are several reasons for the popularity of the gallery. In the cold rainy autumns and winters north of the Alps it was invaluable as a sheltered place for exercise and games; it was well adapted to display the pictures, statuary and bric-à-brac which, in emulation of Italian collectors, the Northern nobles were beginning to acquire; and it showed off to advantage the long line of ancestral portraits and the tapestries representing a succession of episodes from the *Æneid*, the *Orlando Innamorato*, or some of the interminable epics that formed the light reading of the sixteenth century. Then, too, the gallery served for the processions which were a part of the social ceremonial in great houses: the march to the chapel or banquet-hall, the escorting of a royal guest to the state bedroom, and other like pageants.

In France and England the gallery seems for a long time to have been used as a saloon and ball-room, whereas in Italy it was, as a rule, reserved for the display of the art-treasures of the house, no Italian palace worthy of the name being without its gallery of antiquities or of marbles.

In modern houses the ball-room and music-room are the two principal gala apartments. A music-room need not be a gala room in the sense of being used only for large entertainments; but since it is outside the circle of every-day use, and more or less associated with entertaining, it seems best to include it in this chapter.

Many houses of average size have a room large enough for informal entertainments. Such a room, especially in country houses, should be decorated in a gay simple manner in harmony with the rest of the house and with the uses to which the room is to be put. Rooms of this kind may be treated with a white dado, surmounted by walls painted in a pale tint, with boldly modelled garlands and attributes in stucco, also painted white (see Plate XIII). If these stucco decorations are used to frame a series of pictures, such as fruit and flower-pieces or decorative subjects, the effect is especially attractive. Large painted panels with eighteenth-century *genre* subjects or pastoral scenes, set in simple white panelling, are also very decorative. A coved ceiling is best suited to rooms of this comparatively simple character, while in state ball-rooms the dome increases the general appearance of splendor.

XLIII BALL-ROOM

ROYAL PALACE, GENOA. LATE XVIII CENTURY

(EXAMPLE OF STUCCO DECORATION)

Alinari-Art Reference Bureau

XLIV   HALL OF THE HORATII AND THE
CURIATII

PALACE OF THE CONSERVATORS, ROME. XVI CENTURY

(EXAMPLE OF FRESCOED WALLS AND CARVED CEILINGS)

A panelling of mirrors forms a brilliant ball-room decoration, and charming effects are produced by painting these mirrors with birds, butterflies, and garlands of flowers, in the manner of the famous Italian mirror-painter, Mario dei Fiori — "Mario of the Flowers" — as he was called in recognition of his special gift. There is a beautiful room by this artist in the Borghese Palace in Rome, and many Italian palaces contain examples of this peculiarly brilliant style of decoration, which might be revived to advantage by modern painters.

In ball-rooms of great size and importance, where the walls demand a more architectural treatment, the use of an order naturally suggests itself. Pilasters of marble, separated by marble niches containing statues, form a severe but splendid decoration; and if white and colored marbles are combined, and the whole is surmounted by a domed ceiling frescoed in bright colors, the effect is extremely brilliant.

In Italy the architectural decoration of large rooms was often entirely painted (see Plate XLIV), the plaster walls being covered with a fanciful piling-up of statues, porticoes and balustrades, while figures in Oriental costume, or in the masks and particolored dress of the *Comédie Italienne*, leaned from simulated loggias or wandered through marble colonnades.

The Italian decorator held any audacity permissible in a room used only by a throng of people, whose mood and dress made them ready to accept the fairy-tales on the walls as a fitting background to their own masquerading. Modern travellers, walking through these old Italian saloons in the harsh light of day, while cobwebs hang from the audacious architecture, and the cracks in the plaster look like wounds in the cheeks of simpering nymphs and shepherdesses, should remember that such apartments were meant to be seen by the soft light of wax candles in crystal chandeliers, with fantastically dressed dancers thronging the marble floor.

Such a ball-room, if reproduced in the present day, would be far more effective than the conventional white-and-gold room, which, though unobjectionable when well decorated, lacks the imaginative charm, the personal note, given by the painter's touch.

Under Louis XIV many French apartments of state were panelled with colored marbles, with an application of attributes or trophies, and other ornamental motives in fire-gilt bronze: a sumptuous mode of treatment according well with a domed and frescoed ceiling. Tapestry was also much used, and forms an admirable decoration, provided the color-scheme is light and the design animated. Seventeenth and eighteenth-century tapestries are the most suitable, as the scale of color is brighter and the compositions are gayer than in the earlier hangings.

Modern dancers prefer a polished wooden floor, and it is perhaps smoother and more elastic than any other surface; but in beauty and decorative value it cannot be compared with a floor of inlaid marble, and as all the dancing in Italian palaces is still done on such floors, the preference for wood is probably the result of habit. In a ball-room of any importance, especially where marble is used on the walls, the floor should always be of the same substance (see floors in Plates XXIX, XXX, and LV).

Gala apartments, as distinguished from living-rooms, should be lit from the ceiling, never from the walls. No ball-room or saloon is complete without its chandeliers: they are one of the characteristic features of a gala room (see Plates V, XIX, XXXIV, XLIII, XLV, L). For a ball-room, where all should be light and

XLV SALA DELLO ZODIACO

ROYAL PALACE, MANTUA. XVIII CENTURY

(EXAMPLE OF STUCCO DECORATION)

XLVI FRENCH TABLE

(TRANSITION BETWEEN LOUIS XIV AND LOUIS XV PERIODS)

brilliant, rock-crystal or cut-glass chandeliers are most suitable: reflected in a long line of mirrors, they are an invaluable factor in any scheme of gala decoration.

The old French decorators relied upon the reflection of mirrors for producing an effect of distance in the treatment of gala rooms. Above the mantel, there was always a mirror with another of the same shape and size directly opposite; and the glittering perspective thus produced gave to the scene an air of fantastic unreality. The gala suite being so planned that all the rooms adjoined each other, the effect of distance was further enhanced by placing the openings in line, so that on entering the suite it was possible to look down its whole length. The importance of preserving this long vista, or *enfilade*, as the French call it, is dwelt on by all old writers on house-decoration. If a ball-room be properly lit and decorated, it is never necessary to dress it up with any sort of temporary ornamentation: the true mark of the well-decorated ball-room is to look always ready for a ball.

The only chair seen in most modern ball-rooms is the folding camp-seat hired by the hundred when entertainments are given; but there is no reason why a ball-room should be even temporarily disfigured by these makeshifts, which look their worst when an effort is made to conceal their cheap construction under a little gilding and satin. In all old ball-rooms, benches and *tabourets* (small seats without backs) were ranged in a continuous line along the walls. These seats, handsomely designed, and covered with tapestry, velvet, or embroidered silk slips, were a part of the permanent decoration of the room. On ordinary occasions they would be sufficient for a modern ball-room; and when larger entertainments made it needful to provide additional seats, these might be copied from the seventeenth-century *perroquets*, examples of which may be found in the various French works on the history of furniture. These *perroquets,* or folding chairs without arms, made of natural walnut or gilded, with seats of tapestry, velvet or decorated leather, would form an excellent substitute for the modern cotillon seat.

The first rule to be observed in the decoration of the music-room is the avoidance of all stuff hangings, draperies, and substances likely to deaden sound. The treatment chosen for the room must of course depend on its size and its relation to the other rooms in the house. While a music-room should be more subdued in color than a ball-room, sombre tints and heavy ornament are obviously inappropriate: the effect aimed at should be one of lightness and serenity in form and color. However small and simple the music-room may be, it should always appear as though there were space overhead for the notes to escape; and some form of vaulting or doming is therefore more suitable than a flat ceiling.

While plain panelling, if well designed, is never out of keeping, the walls of a music-room are specially suited to a somewhat fanciful style of decoration. In a ball-room, splendor and brilliancy of effect are more needful than a studied delicacy; but where people are seated, and everything in the room is consequently subjected to close and prolonged scrutiny, sprightliness of composition should be combined with variety of detail, the decoration being neither so confused and intricate as to distract attention, nor so conventional as to be dismissed with a glance on entering the room.

The early Renaissance compositions in which stucco low-reliefs blossom into painted arabesques and tendrils, are peculiarly adapted to a small music-room; while those who prefer a more architectural treatment may find admirable examples in some of the Italian eighteenth-century rooms decorated with free-hand stucco ornament, or in the sculptured wood-panelling of the same period in France. At Remiremont in the Vosges, formerly the residence of a noble order of canonesses, the abbess's *hôtel* contains an octagonal music-room of exceptional beauty, the panelled walls being carved with skilfully combined musical instruments and flower-garlands.

In larger apartments a fanciful style of fresco-painting might be employed, as in the rooms painted by Tiepolo in the Villa Valmarana, near Vicenza, or in the staircase of the Palazzo Sina, at Venice, decorated by Longhi with the episodes of an eighteenth-century carnival. Whatever the design chosen, it should never resemble the formal treatment suited to ball-room and saloon: the decoration should sound a note distinctly suggestive of the purpose for which the music-room is used.

It is difficult to understand why modern music-rooms have so long been disfigured by the clumsy lines of grand and upright pianos, since the cases of both might be modified without affecting the construction of the instrument. Of the two, the grand piano would be the easier to remodel: if its elephantine supports were replaced by slender fluted legs, and its case and sounding-board were painted, or inlaid with marquetry, it would resemble the charming old clavecin which preceded the pianoforte.

Fewer changes are possible in the "upright"; but a marked improvement could be produced by straightening its legs and substituting right angles for the weak curves of the lid. The case itself might be made of plainly panelled mahogany, with a few good ormolu ornaments; or of inlaid wood, with a design of musical instruments and similar "attributes"; or it might be decorated with flower-garlands and arabesques painted either on the natural wood or on a gilt or colored background.

Designers should also study the lines of those two long-neglected pieces of furniture, the music-stool and music-stand. The latter should be designed to match the piano, and painted or inlaid like its case. The revolving mushroom that now serves as a music-stool is a modern invention: the old stools were substantial circular seats resting on four fluted legs. The manuals of the eighteenth-century cabinet-makers contain countless models of these piano-seats, which might well be reproduced by modern designers: there seems no practical reason why the accessories of the piano should be less decorative than those of the harpsichord.

XLVII LIBRARY OF LOUIS XVI

PALACE OF VERSAILLES

(LOUIS XV ROLL-TOP DESK)

Giraudon

XLVIII   SMALL LIBRARY AT AUDLEY END, ENGLAND

XVIII CENTURY

National Monuments Record

XII

THE LIBRARY, SMOKING-ROOM, AND "DEN"

IN the days when furniture was defined as "that which may be carried about," the natural bookcase was a chest with a strong lock. These chests, packed with precious manuscripts, followed the prince or noble from one castle to another, and were even carried after him into camp. Before the invention of printing, when twenty or thirty books formed an exceptionally large library, and many great personages were content with the possession of one volume, such ambulant bookcases were sufficient for the requirements of the most eager bibliophile. Occasionally the volumes were kept in a small press or cupboard, and placed in a chest only when their owner travelled; but the bookcase, as now known, did not take shape until much later, for when books multiplied with the introduction of printing, it became customary to fit up for their reception little rooms called *cabinets*. In the famous *cabinet* of Catherine de' Medici at Blois the walls are lined with bookshelves concealed behind sliding panels — a contrivance rendered doubly necessary by the general insecurity of property, and by the fact that the books of that period, whether in manuscript or printed, were made sumptuous as church jewelry by the art of painter and goldsmith.

Long after the establishment of the printing-press, books, except in the hands of the scholar, continued to be a kind of curiosity, like other objects of art: less an intellectual need than a treasure upon which rich men prided themselves. It was not until the middle of the seventeenth century that the taste for books became a taste for reading. France led the way in this new fashion, which was assiduously cultivated in those Parisian *salons* of which Madame de Rambouillet's is the recognized type. The possession of a library, hitherto the privilege of kings, of wealthy monasteries, or of some distinguished patron of letters like Grolier, Maioli, or de Thou, now came to be regarded as a necessity of every gentleman's establishment. Beautiful bindings were still highly valued, and some of the most wonderful work produced in France belongs to the seventeenth and eighteenth centuries; but as people began to buy books for the sake of what they contained, less exaggerated importance was attached to their exterior, so that bindings, though perfect as taste and skill could make them, were seldom as extravagantly enriched as in the two preceding centuries. Up to a certain point this change was not to be regretted: the mediæval book, with its gold or ivory bas-reliefs bordered with precious stones, and its massive jewelled clasps, was more like a monstrance or reliquary than anything meant for less ceremonious use. It remained for the Italian printers and binders of the sixteenth century, and for their French imitators, to adapt the form of the book to its purpose, changing, as it were, a jewelled idol to a human companion.

The substitution of the octavo for the folio, and certain modifications in binding which made it possible to stand books upright instead of laying one above the other with edges outward, gradually gave to the library a more modern aspect. In France, by the middle of the seventeenth century, the library had come to be a recognized feature in private houses. The Renaissance *cabinet* continued to be the common receptacle for books; but as the shelves were no longer concealed, bindings now contributed to the decoration of the room. Movable bookcases were not unknown, but these seem to have been merely presses in which wooden door-panels were replaced by glass or by a lattice-work of brass wire. The typical French bookcase *à deux corps* — that is, made in two separate parts, the lower a cupboard to contain prints and folios, the upper with shelves and glazed or latticed doors — was introduced later, and is still the best model for a movable book-case. In rooms of any importance, however, the French architect always preferred to build his book-shelves into niches formed in the thickness of the wall, thus utilizing the books as part of his scheme of decoration.

There is no doubt that this is not only the most practical, but the most decorative, way of housing any collection of books large enough to be so employed. To adorn the walls of a library, and then conceal their ornamentation by expensive bookcases, is a waste, or rather a misapplication, of effects — always a sin against æsthetic principles.

The importance of bookbindings as an element in house-decoration has already been touched upon; but since a taste for good bindings has come to be regarded as a collector's fad, like accumulating snuff-boxes or *baisers-de-paix*, it seems needful to point out how obvious and valuable a means of decoration is lost by disregarding the outward appearance of books. To be decorative, a bookcase need not contain the productions of the master-binders, — old volumes by Eve and Derôme, or the work of Roger Payne and Sanderson, — unsurpassed as they are in color-value. Ordinary bindings of half morocco or vellum form an expanse of warm lustrous color; such bindings are comparatively inexpensive; yet people will often hesitate to pay for a good edition bound in plain levant half the amount they are ready to throw away upon a piece of modern Saxe or a silver photograph-frame.

The question of binding leads incidentally to that of editions, though the latter is hardly within the scope of this book. People who have begun to notice the outside of their books naturally come to appreciate paper and type; and thus learn that the modern book is too often merely the cheapest possible vehicle for putting words into print. The last few years have brought about some improvement; and it is now not unusual for a publisher, in bringing out a book at the ordinary rates, to produce also a small edition in large-paper copies. These large-paper books, though as yet far from perfect in type and make-up, are superior to the average "commercial article"; and, apart from their artistic merit, are in themselves a good investment, since the value of such editions increases steadily year by year. Those who cannot afford both edition and binding will do better to buy large-paper books or current first editions in boards, than "handsomely bound" volumes unworthy in type and paper. The plain paper or buckram covers of a good publisher are, in fact, more decorative, because more artistic, than showy tree-calf or "antique morocco."

The same principle applies to the library itself: plain shelves filled with good editions in good bindings are more truly decorative than ornate bookcases lined with tawdry books.

It has already been pointed out that the plan of building bookshelves into the walls is the most decorative and the most practical (see Plate XLVIII). The best examples of this treatment are found in France. The walls of the rooms thus decorated were usually of panelled wood, either in natural oak or walnut, as in the beautiful library of the old university at Nancy, or else painted in two contrasting colors, such as gray and white. When not set in recesses, the shelves formed a sort of continuous lining around the walls, as in the library of Louis XVI in the palace at Versailles (see Plate XLVII), or in that of the Duc de Choiseul at Chanteloup, now set up in one of the rooms of the public library at Tours.

In either case, instead of being detached pieces of furniture, the bookcases formed an organic part of the wall-decoration. Any study of old French works on house-decoration and furniture will show how seldom the detached bookcase was used in French libraries: but few models are to be found, and these were probably designed for use in the boudoir or study, rather than in the library proper (see bookcase in Plate V).

In England, where private libraries were fewer and less extensive, the movable bookcase was much used, and examples of built-in shelves are proportionately rarer. The hand-books of the old English cabinet-makers contain innumerable models of handsome bookcases, with glazed doors set with diamond-shaped panes in wooden mouldings, and the familiar broken pediment surmounted by a bust or an urn. It was natural that where books were few, small bookcases should be preferred to a room lined with shelves; and in the seventeenth century, according to John Evelyn, the "three nations of Great Britain" contained fewer books than Paris.

Almost all the old bookcases had one feature in common: that is, the lower cupboard with solid doors. The bookcase proper rested upon this projecting cupboard, thus raising the books above the level of the furniture. The prevalent fashion of low book-shelves, starting from the floor, and not extending much higher than the dado-moulding, has probably been brought about by the other recent fashion of low-studded rooms.   Architects are beginning to rediscover the forgotten fact that the stud of a room should be regulated by the dimensions of its floor-space; so that in the newer houses the dwarf bookcase is no longer a necessity. It is certainly less convenient than the tall old-fashioned press; for not only must one kneel to reach the lower shelves, but the books are hidden, and access to them is obstructed, by their being on a level with the furniture.

The general decoration of the library should be of such character as to form a background or setting to the books, rather than to distract attention from them.   The richly adorned room in which books are but a minor incident is, in fact, no library at all.   There is no reason why the decorations of a library should not be splendid; but in that case the books must be splendid too, and sufficient in number to dominate all the accessory decorations of the room.

When there are books enough, it is best to use them as part of the decorative treatment of the walls, panelling any intervening spaces in a severe and dignified style; otherwise movable bookcases may be placed against the more important wall-spaces, the walls being decorated with wooden panelling or with mouldings and stucco ornaments; but in this case composition and color-scheme must be so subdued as to throw the bookcases and their contents into marked relief.   It does not follow that because books are the chief feature of the library, other ornaments should be excluded; but they should be used with discrimination, and so chosen as to harmonize with the spirit of the room.   Nowhere is the modern litter of knick-knacks and photographs more inappropriate than in the library.   The tables should be large, substantial, and clear of everything but lamps, books and papers — one table

XLIX WRITING-CHAIR

LOUIS XV PERIOD

The Metropolitan Museum of Art, Gift of J. Pierpont Morgan, 1906

L DINING-ROOM

PALACE OF COMPIÈGNE. LOUIS XVI PERIOD

(OVER-DOORS AND OVER-MANTEL PAINTED IN GRISAILLE, BY SAUVAGE)

at least being given over to the filing of books and newspapers. The library writing-table is seldom large enough, or sufficiently free from odds and ends in the shape of photograph-frames, silver boxes, and flower-vases, to give free play to the elbows. A large solid table of the kind called *bureau-ministre* (see the table in Plate XLVII) is well adapted to the library; and in front of it should stand a comfortable writing-chair such as that represented in Plate XLIX.

The housing of a great private library is one of the most interesting problems of interior architecture. Such a room, combining monumental dimensions with the rich color-values and impressive effect produced by tiers of fine bindings, affords unequalled opportunity for the exercise of the architect's skill. The two-storied room with gallery and stairs and domed or vaulted ceiling is the finest setting for a great collection. Space may of course be gained by means of a series of bookcases projecting into the room and forming deep bays along each of the walls; but this arrangement is seldom necessary save in a public library, and however skilfully handled must necessarily diminish the architectural effect of the room. In America the great private library is still so much a thing of the future that its treatment need not be discussed in detail. Few of the large houses lately built in the United States contain a library in the serious meaning of the term; but it is to be hoped that the next generation of architects will have wider opportunities in this direction.

The smoking-room proper, with its *mise en scène* of Turkish divans, narghilehs, brass coffee-trays, and other Oriental properties, is no longer considered a necessity in the modern house; and the room which would formerly have been used for this special purpose now comes rather under the head of the master's lounging-room, or "den"— since the latter word seems to have attained the dignity of a technical term.

Whatever extravagances the upholsterer may have committed in other parts of the house, it is usually conceded that common sense should regulate the furnishing of the den. Fragile chairs, lace-petticoat lamp-shades and irrelevant bric-à-brac are consequently excluded; and the master's sense of comfort often expresses itself in a set of "office" furniture — a roller-top desk, a revolving chair, and others of the puffy type already described as the accepted model of a luxurious seat. Thus freed from the superfluous, the den is likely to be the most comfortable room in the house; and the natural inference is that a room, in order to be comfortable, must be ugly. One can picture the derision of the man who is told that he might, without the smallest sacrifice of comfort or convenience, transact his business at a Louis XVI writing-table, seated in a Louis XVI chair! — yet the handsomest desks of the last century — the fine old *bureaux à la Kaunitz* or *à cylindre* — were the prototypes of the modern "roller-top"; and the cane or leather-seated writing-chair, with rounded back and five slim strong legs, was far more comfortable than the amorphous revolving seat. Convenience was not sacrificed to beauty in either desk or chair; but both the old pieces, being designed by skilled cabinet-makers, were as decorative as they were useful. There seems, in fact, no reason why the modern den should not resemble the financiers' *bureaux* seen in so many old prints: rooms of dignified plainness, but where each line of wall-panelling and furniture was as carefully studied and intelligently adapted to its ends as though intended for a drawing-room or boudoir.

Reference has been made to the way in which, even in small houses, a room may be sacrificed to a supposed "effect," or to some inherited tradition as to its former use. Thus the family drawing-room is too often made uninhabitable from some vague feeling that a "drawing-room" is not worthy of its name unless too fine to sit in; while the small front room on the ground floor — in the average American house the only corner given over to the master — is thrown into the hall, either that the house may appear larger and handsomer, or from sheer inability to make so small a room habitable.

There is no reason why even a ten-by-twelve or an eight-by-fourteen foot room should not be made comfortable; and the following suggestions are intended to indicate the lines on which an appropriate scheme of decoration might be carried out.

In most town houses the small room down-stairs is built with an opening in the longitudinal wall, close to the front door, while there is usually another entrance at the back of the room, facing the window; one at least of these openings being, as a rule, of exaggerated width. In such cases the door in the side of the room should be walled up: this gives privacy and provides enough additional wall-space for a good-sized piece of furniture.

The best way of obtaining an effect of size is to panel the walls by means of clear-cut architectural mouldings : a few strong vertical lines will give dignity to the room and height to the ceiling. The walls should be free from pattern and light in color, since dark walls necessitate much artificial light, and have the disadvantage of making a room look small.

The ceiling, if not plain, must be ornamented with the lightest tracery, and supported by a cornice correspondingly simple in design. Heavy ceiling-mouldings are obviously out of place in a small room, and a plain expanse of plaster is always preferable to misapplied ornament.

A single curtain made of some flexible material, such as corduroy or thin unlined damask, and so hung that it may be readily drawn back during the day, is sufficient for the window; while in a corner near this window may be placed an easy-chair and a small solidly made table, large enough to hold a lamp and a book or two.

These rooms, in some recently built town houses, contain chimneys set in an angle of the wall: a misplaced attempt at quaintness, making it inconvenient to sit near the hearth, and seriously interfering with the general arrangement of the room. When the chimney occupies the centre of the longitudinal wall there is space, even in a very narrow room, for a group of chairs about the fireplace — provided, as we are now supposing, the opening in the parallel wall has been closed. A bookcase or some other high piece of furniture may be placed on each side of the mantel, and there will be space opposite for a sofa and a good-sized writing-table. If the pieces of furniture chosen are in scale with the dimensions of the room, and are placed against the wall, instead of being set sideways, with the usual easel or palm-tree behind them, it is surprising to see how much a small room may contain without appearing to be overcrowded.

XIII

THE DINING-ROOM

THE dining-room, as we know it, is a comparatively recent innovation in house-planning. In the early middle ages the noble and his retainers ate in the hall; then the *grand'salle*, built for ceremonial uses, began to serve as a banqueting-room, while the meals eaten in private were served in the lord's chamber. As house-planning adapted itself to the growing complexity of life, the mediæval bedroom developed into a private suite of living-rooms, preceded by an antechamber; and this antechamber, or one of the small adjoining cabinets, was used as the family dining-room, the banqueting-hall being still reserved for state entertainments.

The plan of dining at haphazard in any of the family living-rooms persisted on the Continent until the beginning of the eighteenth century: even then it was comparatively rare, in France, to see a room set apart for the purpose of dining. In small *hôtels* and apartments, people continued to dine in the antechamber; where there were two antechambers, the inner was used for that purpose; and it was only in grand houses, or in the luxurious establishments of the *femmes galantes*, that dining-rooms were to be found. Even in such cases the room described as a *salle à manger* was often only a central antechamber or saloon into which the living-rooms opened; indeed, Madame du Barry's sumptuous dining-

room at Luciennes was a vestibule giving directly upon the
peristyle of the villa.

In England the act of dining seems to have been taken more
seriously, while the rambling outgrowths of the Elizabethan
residence included a greater variety of rooms than could be contained in any but the largest houses built on more symmetrical
lines. Accordingly, in old English house-plans we find rooms
designated as "dining-parlors"; many houses, in fact, contained
two or three, each with a different exposure, so that they might
be used at different seasons. These rooms can hardly be said to
represent our modern dining-room, since they were not planned
in connection with kitchen and offices, and were probably
used as living-rooms when not needed for dining. Still, it was
from the Elizabethan dining-parlor that the modern dining-room
really developed; and so recently has it been specialized into a
room used only for eating, that a generation ago old-fashioned
people in England and America habitually used their dining-rooms
to sit in. On the Continent the incongruous uses of the rooms
in which people dined made it necessary that the furniture should
be easily removed. In the middle ages, people dined at long
tables composed of boards resting on trestles, while the seats
were narrow wooden benches or stools, so constructed that they
could easily be carried away when the meal was over. With the
sixteenth century, the *table-à-tréteaux* gave way to various folding tables with legs, and the wooden stools were later replaced
by folding seats without arms, called *perroquets*. In the middle
ages, when banquets were given in the *grand'salle*, the plate was
displayed on movable shelves covered with a velvet slip, or on
elaborately carved dressers; but on ordinary occasions little silver
was set out in French dining-rooms, and the great English side-

LI DINING-ROOM FOUNTAIN

PALACE OF FONTAINEBLEAU. LOUIS XV PERIOD

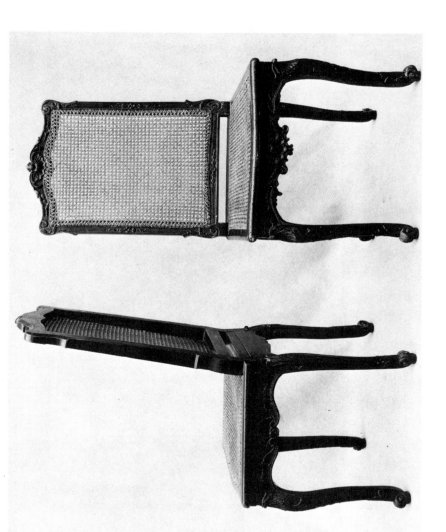

LII DINING-CHAIR

LOUIS XIV PERIOD

The Metropolitan Museum of Art, Gift of J. Pierpont Morgan, 1906

board, with its array of urns, trays and wine-coolers, was unknown in France. In the common antechamber dining-room,
whatever was needed for the table was kept in a press or cupboard with solid wooden doors; changes of service being carried
on by means of serving-tables, or *servantes* — narrow marble-
topped consoles ranged against the walls of the room.

For examples of dining-rooms, as we understand the term, one
must look to the grand French houses of the eighteenth century
(see Plate L) and to the same class of dwellings in England. In
France such dining-rooms were usually intended for gala entertainments, the family being still served in antechamber or cabinet;
but English houses of the same period generally contain a family
dining-room and another intended for state.

The dining-room of Madame du Barry at Luciennes, already
referred to, was a magnificent example of the great dining-saloon.
The ceiling was a painted Olympus; the white marble walls were
subdivided by Corinthian pilasters with plinths and capitals of
gilt bronze, surmounted by a frieze of bas-reliefs framed in gold;
four marble niches contained statues by Pajou, Lecomte, and
Moineau; and the general brilliancy of effect was increased by
crystal chandeliers, hung in the intercolumniations against a background of looking-glass.

Such a room, the banqueting-hall of the official mistress, represents the *courtisane's* ideal of magnificence: decorations as splendid, but more sober and less theatrical, marked the dining-rooms
of the aristocracy, as at Choisy, Gaillon and Rambouillet.

The state dining-rooms of the eighteenth century were often
treated with an order, niches with statues being placed between
the pilasters. Sometimes one of these niches contained a fountain serving as a wine-cooler — a survival of the stone or metal

wall-fountains in which dishes were washed in the mediæval dining-room. Many of these earlier fountains had been merely fixed to the wall; but those of the eighteenth century, though varying greatly in design, were almost always an organic part of the wall-decoration (see Plate LI). Sometimes, in apartments of importance, they formed the pedestal of a life-size group or statue, as in the dining-room of Madame de Pompadour; while in smaller rooms they consisted of a semicircular basin of marble projecting from the wall and surmounted by groups of cupids, dolphins or classic attributes. The banqueting-gallery of Trianon-sous-Bois contains in one of its longitudinal walls two wide niches with long marble basins; and Mariette's edition of d'Aviler's *Cours d'Architecture* gives the elevation of a recessed buffet flanked by small niches containing fountains. The following description, accompanying d'Aviler's plate, is quoted here as an instance of the manner in which elaborate compositions were worked out by the old decorators: " The second antechamber, being sometimes used as a dining-room, is a suitable place for the buffet represented. This buffet, which may be incrusted with marble or stone, or panelled with wood-work, consists in a recess occupying one of the side walls of the room. The recess contains a shelf of marble or stone, supported on brackets and surmounting a small stone basin which serves as a wine-cooler. Above the shelf is an attic flanked by volutes, and over this attic may be placed a picture, generally a flower or fruit-piece, or the representation of a concert, or some such agreeable scene; while in the accompanying plate the attic is crowned by a bust of Comus, wreathed with vines by two little satyrs — the group detaching itself against a trellised background enlivened with birds. The composition is completed by two lateral niches

LIII DINING-CHAIR

LOUIS XVI PERIOD

The Metropolitan Museum of Art, Purchase, Rogers Fund, 1923

LIV BEDROOM

PALACE OF FONTAINEBLEAU. LOUIS XIV PERIOD

(LOUIS XVI BED AND CHAIR, MODERN SOFA)

Arch. Phot. Paris

for fountains, adorned with masks, tritons and dolphins of
gilded lead."

These built-in sideboards and fountains were practically the
only feature distinguishing the old dining-rooms from other gala
apartments. At a period when all rooms were painted, panelled,
or hung with tapestry, no special style of decoration was thought
needful for the dining-room; though tapestry was seldom used,
for the practical reason that stuff hangings are always objectionable in a room intended for eating.

Towards the end of the seventeenth century, when comfortable
seats began to be made, an admirably designed dining-room chair
replaced the earlier benches and *perroquets*. The eighteenth century dining-chair is now often confounded with the light *chaise
volante* used in drawing-rooms, and cabinet-makers frequently
sell the latter as copies of old dining-chairs. These were in fact
much heavier and more comfortable, and whether cane-seated or
upholstered, were invariably made with wide deep seats, so that
the long banquets of the day might be endured without constraint
or fatigue; while the backs were low and narrow, in order not to
interfere with the service of the table. (See Plates LII and LIII.
Plates XLVI and L also contain good examples of dining-chairs.)
In England the state dining-room was decorated much as it was
in France: the family dining-room was simply a plain parlor, with
wide mahogany sideboards or tall glazed cupboards for the display
of plate and china. The solid English dining-chairs of mahogany,
if less graceful than those used on the Continent, are equally well
adapted to their purpose.

The foregoing indications may serve to suggest the lines upon
which dining-room decoration might be carried out in the present
day. The avoidance of all stuff hangings and heavy curtains is

of great importance: it will be observed that even window-curtains were seldom used in old dining-rooms, such care being given to the decorative detail of window and embrasure that they needed no additional ornament in the way of drapery. A bare floor of stone or marble is best suited to the dining-room; but where the floor is covered, it should be with a rug, not with a nailed-down carpet.

The dining-room should be lit by wax candles in side *appliques* or in a chandelier; and since anything tending to produce heat and to exhaust air is especially objectionable in a room used for eating, the walls should be sufficiently light in color to make little artificial light necessary. In the dining-rooms of the last century, in England as well as on the Continent, the color-scheme was usually regulated by this principle: the dark dining-room panelled with mahogany or hung with sombre leather is an invention of our own times. It has already been said that the old family dining-room was merely a panelled parlor. Sometimes the panels were of light unvarnished oak, but oftener they were painted in white or in some pale tint easily lit by wax candles. The walls were often hung with fruit or flower-pieces, or with pictures of fish and game: a somewhat obvious form of adornment which it has long been the fashion to ridicule, but which was not without decorative value and appropriateness. Pictures representing life and action often grow tiresome when looked at over and over again, day after day: a fact which the old decorators probably had in mind when they hung what the French call *natures mortes* in the dining-room.

Concerning the state dining-room that forms a part of many modern houses little remains to be said beyond the descriptions already given of the various gala apartments. It is obvious that the banqueting-hall should be less brilliant than a ball-room and less fanciful in decoration than a music-room: a severer and more restful treatment naturally suggests itself, but beyond this no special indications are required.

The old dining-rooms were usually heated by porcelain stoves. Such a stove, of fine architectural design, set in a niche corresponding with that which contains the fountain, is of great decorative value in the composition of the room; and as it has the advantage of giving out less concentrated heat than an open fire, it is specially well suited to a small or narrow dining-room, where some of the guests must necessarily sit close to the hearth.

Most houses which have banquet-halls contain also a smaller apartment called a breakfast-room; but as this generally corresponds in size and usage with the ordinary family dining-room, the same style of decoration is applicable to both. However ornate the banquet-hall may be, the breakfast-room must of course be simple and free from gilding: the more elaborate the decorations of the larger room, the more restful such a contrast will be found.

Of the dinner-table, as we now know it, little need be said. The ingenious but ugly extension-table with a central support, now used all over the world, is an English invention. There seems no reason why the general design should not be improved without interfering with the mechanism of this table; but of course it can never be so satisfactory to the eye as one of the old round or square tables, with four or six tapering legs, such as were used in eighteenth-century dining-rooms before the introduction of the "extension."

XIV

BEDROOMS

THE history of the bedroom has been incidentally touched upon in tracing the development of the drawing-room from the mediæval hall. It was shown that early in the middle ages the sleeping-chamber, which had been one of the first outgrowths of the hall, was divided into the *chambre de parade*, or incipient drawing-room, and the *chambre au giste*, or actual sleeping-room.

The increasing development of social life in the sixteenth century brought about a further change; the state bedroom being set aside for entertainments of ceremony, while the sleeping-chamber was used as the family living-room and as the scene of suppers, card-parties, and informal receptions — or sometimes actually as the kitchen. Indeed, so varied were the uses to which the *chambre au giste* was put, that in France especially it can hardly be said to have offered a refuge from the promiscuity of the hall.

As a rule, the bedrooms of the Renaissance and of the seventeenth century were very richly furnished. The fashion of raising the bed on a dais separated from the rest of the room by columns and a balustrade was introduced in France in the time of Louis XIV. This innovation gave rise to the habit of dividing the decoration of the room into two parts; the walls being usually panelled or painted, while the "alcove," as it was called, was hung in tapestry, velvet, or some rich stuff in keeping with the heavy curtains that completely enveloped the bedstead. This use of stuff hangings about the bed, so contrary to our ideas of bedroom hygiene, was due to the difficulty of heating the large high-studded rooms of the period, and also, it must be owned, to the prevalent dread of fresh air as of something essentially unwholesome and pernicious.

In the early middle ages people usually slept on the floor; though it would seem that occasionally, to avoid cold or dampness, the mattress was laid on cords stretched upon a low wooden framework. In the fourteenth century the use of such frameworks became more general, and the bed was often enclosed in curtains hung from a tester resting on four posts. Bed-hangings and coverlet were often magnificently embroidered; but in order that it might not be necessary to transport from place to place the unwieldy bedstead and tester, these were made in the rudest manner, without attempt at carving or adornment. In course of time this primitive framework developed into the sumptuous four-post bedstead of the Renaissance, with elaborately carved cornice and *colonnes torses* enriched with gilding. Thenceforward more wealth and skill were expended upon the bedstead than upon any other article of furniture. Gilding, carving, and inlaying of silver, ivory or mother-of-pearl, combined to adorn the framework, and embroidery made the coverlet and hangings resplendent as church vestments. This magnificence is explained by the fact that it was customary for the lady of the house to lie in bed while receiving company. In many old prints representing suppers, card-parties, or afternoon visits, the hostess is thus seen, with elaborately dressed head and stiff brocade gown, while her friends are grouped about the bedside in equally rich attire.

This curious custom persisted until late in the eighteenth century; and under such conditions it was natural that the old cabinet-makers should vie with each other in producing a variety of ornate and fanciful bedsteads. It would be useless to enumerate here the modifications in design marking the different periods of decoration: those who are interested in the subject will find it treated in detail in the various French works on furniture.

It was natural that while the bedroom was used as a *salon* it should be decorated with more elaboration than would otherwise have been fitting; but two causes combined to simplify its treatment in the eighteenth century. One of these was the new fashion of *petits appartements*. With artists so keenly alive to proportion as the old French designers, it was inevitable that such a change in dimensions should bring about a corresponding change in decoration. The bedrooms of the eighteenth century, though sometimes elaborate in detail, had none of the pompous richness of the great Renaissance or Louis XIV room (see Plate LIV). The pretentious dais with its screen of columns was replaced by a niche containing the bed; plain wood-panelling succeeded to tapestry and embroidered hangings; and the heavy carved ceiling with its mythological centre-picture made way for light traceries on plaster.

The other change in the decoration of French bedrooms was due to the substitution of linen or cotton bed and window-hangings for the sumptuous velvets and brocades of the seventeenth century. This change has usually been ascribed to the importation of linens and cottons from the East; and no doubt the novelty of these gay *indiennes* stimulated the taste for simple hangings. The old inventories, however, show that, in addition to the imported India hangings, plain white linen curtains with a colored border were much used; and it is probably the change in the size of rooms that first led to the adoption of thin washable hangings. The curtains and bed-draperies of damask or brocatelle, so well suited to the high-studded rooms of the seventeenth century, would have been out of place in the small apartments of the Regency. In studying the history of decoration, it will generally be found that the supposed vagaries of house-furnishing were actually based on some practical requirement; and in this instance the old decorators were doubtless guided rather by common sense than by caprice. The adoption of these washable materials certainly introduced a style of bedroom-furnishing answering to all the requirements of recent hygiene; for not only were windows and bedsteads hung with unlined cotton or linen, but chairs and sofas were covered with removable *housses*, or slip-covers; while the painted wall-panelling and bare brick or parquet floors came far nearer to the modern sanitary ideal than do the papered walls and nailed-down carpets still seen in many bedrooms. This simple form of decoration had the additional charm of variety; for it was not unusual to have several complete sets of curtains and slip-covers, embroidered to match, and changed with the seasons. The hangings and covers of the queen's bedroom at Versailles were changed four times a year.

Although bedrooms are still " done " in chintz, and though of late especially there has been a reaction from the satin-damask bedroom with its dust-collecting upholstery and knick-knacks, the modern habit of lining chintz curtains and of tufting chairs has done away with the chief advantages of the simpler style of treatment. There is something illogical in using washable stuffs in such a way that they cannot be washed, especially in view of the fact that the heavily lined curtains, which might be useful to exclude light and cold, are in nine cases out of ten so hung by the upholsterer that they cannot possibly be drawn at night.   Besides, the patterns of modern chintzes have so little in common with the *toiles imprimées* of the seventeenth and eighteenth centuries that they scarcely serve the same decorative purpose; and it is therefore needful to give some account of the old French bedroom hangings, as well as of the manner in which they were employed.

The liking for *cotonnades* showed itself in France early in the seventeenth century.   Before this, cotton materials had been imported from the East; but in the seventeenth century a manufactory was established in France, and until about 1800 cotton and linen curtains and furniture-coverings remained in fashion.   This taste was encouraged by the importation of the *toiles des Indes,* printed cottons of gay color and fanciful design, much sought after in France, especially after the government, in order to protect native industry, had restricted the privilege of importing them to the *Compagnie des Indes.*   It was not until Oberkampf established his manufactory at Jouy in 1760 that the French *toiles* began to replace those of foreign manufacture.   Hitherto the cottons made in France had been stamped merely in outline, the colors being filled in by hand; but Oberkampf invented a method of printing in colors, thereby making France the leading market for such stuffs.

The earliest printed cottons having been imported from India and China, it was natural that the style of the Oriental designers should influence their European imitators.   Europe had, in fact, been prompt to recognize the singular beauty of Chinese art, and in France the passion for *chinoiseries*, first aroused by Mazarin's collection of Oriental objects of art, continued unabated until the general decline of taste at the end of the eighteenth century.   Nowhere, perhaps, was the influence of Chinese art more beneficial to European designers than in the composition of stuff-patterns. The fantastic gaiety and variety of Chinese designs, in which the human figure so largely predominates, gave fresh animation to European compositions, while the absence of perspective and modelling preserved that conventionalism so essential in pattern-designing. The voluminous acanthus-leaves, the fleur-de-lys, arabesques and massive scroll-work so suitable to the Genoese velvets and Lyons silks of the sixteenth and seventeenth centuries, would have been far too magnificent for the cotton stuffs that were beginning to replace those splendid tissues. On a thin material a heavy architectural pattern was obviously inappropriate; besides, it would have been out of scale with the smaller rooms and lighter style of decoration then coming into fashion.

The French designer, while influenced by Chinese compositions, was too artistic to be satisfied with literal reproductions of his Oriental models. Absorbing the spirit of the Chinese designs, he either blent mandarins and pagodas with Italian grottoes, French landscapes, and classical masks and trophies, in one of those delightful inventions which are the fairy-tales of decorative art, or applied the principles of Oriental design to purely European subjects. In comparing the printed cottons of the seventeenth and eighteenth centuries with modern chintzes, it will be seen that the latter are either covered with monotonous repetitions of a geometrical figure, or with realistic reproductions of some natural object. Many wall-papers and chintzes of the present day represent loose branches of flowers scattered on a plain surface, with no more relation to each other or to their background than so many real flowers fixed at random against the wall. This literal rendering of natural objects with deceptive accuracy, always condemned by the best artists, is especially inappropriate when brought in close contact with the highly conventionalized forms of architectural composition. In this respect, the endlessly repeated geometrical figure is obviously less objectionable; yet the geometrical design, as produced to-day, has one defect in common with the other — that is, lack of imagination. Modern draughtsmen, in eliminating from their work that fanciful element (always strictly subordinated to some general scheme of composition) which marked the designs of the last two centuries, have deprived themselves of the individuality and freshness that might have saved their patterns from monotony.

This rejection of the fanciful in composition is probably due to the excessive use of pattern in modern decoration. Where much pattern is used, it must be as monotonous as possible, or it will become unbearable. The old decorators used few lines, and permitted themselves more freedom in design ; or rather they remembered, what is now too often forgotten, that in the decoration of a room furniture and objects of art help to make design, and in consequence they were chiefly concerned with providing plain spaces of background to throw into relief the contents of the room. Of late there has been so marked a return to plain panelled or painted walls that the pattern-designer will soon be encouraged to give freer rein to his fancy. In a room where walls and floor are of uniform tint, there is no reason why the design of curtains and chair-coverings should consist of long straight rows of buttercups or crocuses, endlessly repeated.

It must not be thought that the old designs were unconventional. Nature, in passing through the medium of the imagination, is necessarily transposed and in a manner conventionalized; and it is this transposition, this deliberate selection of certain

LV BATH-ROOM

PITTI PALACE, FLORENCE. LATE XVIII CENTURY

(DECORATED BY CACIALLI)

Alinari-Art Reference Bureau

LVI BRONZE ANDIRON (VENETIAN SCHOOL)

XVI CENTURY

characteristics to the exclusion of others, that distinguishes the work of art from a cast or a photograph. But the reduction of natural objects to geometrical forms is only one of the results of artistic selection. The Italian fresco-painters — the recognized masters of wall-decoration in the flat — always used the naturalistic method, but subject to certain restrictions in composition or color. This applies also to the Chinese designers, and to the humbler European pattern-makers who on more modest lines followed the same sound artistic traditions. In studying the *toiles peintes* manufactured in Europe previous to the present century, it will be seen that where the design included the human figure or landscape naturalistically treated (as in the fables of Æsop and La Fontaine, or the history of Don Quixote), the pattern was either printed entirely in one color, or so fantastically colored that by no possibility could it pass for an attempt at a literal rendering of nature. Besides, in all such compositions (and here the Chinese influence is seen) perspective was studiously avoided, and the little superimposed groups or scenes were either connected by some decorative arabesque, or so designed that by their outline they formed a recurring pattern. On the other hand, when the design was obviously conventional a variety of colors was freely used. The introduction of the human figure, animals, architecture and landscape into stuff-patterns undoubtedly gave to the old designs an animation lacking in those of the present day; and a return to the *pays bleu* of the Chinese artist would be a gain to modern decoration.

Of the various ways in which a bedroom may be planned, none is so luxurious and practical as the French method of subdividing it into a suite composed of two or more small rooms. Where space is not restricted there should in fact be four rooms, preceded by an antechamber separating the suite from the main corridor of the house. The small sitting-room or boudoir opens into this antechamber; and next comes the bedroom, beyond which are the dressing and bath rooms. In French suites of this kind there are usually but two means of entrance from the main corridor: one for the use of the occupant, leading into the antechamber, the other opening into the bath-room, to give access to the servants. This arrangement, besides giving greater privacy, preserves much valuable wall-space, which would be sacrificed in America to the supposed necessity of making every room in a house open upon one of the main passageways.

The plan of the bedroom suite can of course be carried out only in large houses; but even where there is no lack of space, such an arrangement is seldom adopted by American architects, and most of the more important houses recently built contain immense bedrooms, instead of a series of suites. To enumerate the practical advantages of the suite over the single large room hardly comes within the scope of this book; but as the uses to which a bedroom is put fall into certain natural subdivisions, it will be more convenient to consider it as a suite.

Since bedrooms are no longer used as *salons*, there is no reason for decorating them in an elaborate manner; and, however magnificent the other apartments, it is evident that in this part of the house simplicity is most fitting. Now that people have been taught the unhealthiness of sleeping in a room with stuff hangings, heavy window-draperies and tufted furniture, the old fashion of painted walls and bare floors naturally commends itself; and as the bedroom suite is but the subdivision of one large room, it is obviously better that the same style of decoration should be used throughout.

For this reason, plain panelled walls and chintz or cotton hangings are more appropriate to the boudoir than silk and gilding. If the walls are without pattern, a figured chintz may be chosen for curtains and furniture ; while those who prefer plain tints should use unbleached cotton, trimmed with bands of color, or some colored linen with applications of gimp or embroidery. It is a good plan to cover all the chairs and sofas in the bedroom suite with slips matching the window-curtains; but where this is done, the furniture should, if possible, be designed for the purpose, since the lines of modern upholstered chairs are not suited to slips. The habit of designing furniture for slip-covers originated in the middle ages. At a time when the necessity of transporting furniture was added to the other difficulties of travel, it was usual to have common carpenter-built benches and tables, that might be left behind without risk, and to cover these with richly embroidered slips. The custom persisted long after furniture had ceased to be a part of luggage, and the benches and *tabourets* now seen in many European palaces are covered merely with embroidered slips. Even when a set of furniture was upholstered with silk, it was usual, in the eighteenth century, to provide embroidered cotton covers for use in summer, while curtains of the same stuff were substituted for the heavier hangings used in winter. Old inventories frequently mention these *tentures d'été*, which are well adapted to our hot summer climate.

The boudoir should contain a writing-table, a lounge or *lit de repos*, and one or two comfortable arm-chairs, while in a bedroom forming part of a suite only the bedstead and its accessories should be placed.

The pieces of furniture needed in a well-appointed dressing-room are the toilet-table, wash-stand, clothes-press and cheval-glass, with the addition, if space permits, of one or two commodes or chiffonniers. The designing of modern furniture of this kind is seldom satisfactory; yet many who are careful to choose simple, substantial pieces for the other rooms of the house, submit to the pretentious "bedroom suit" of bird's-eye maple or mahogany, with its wearisome irrelevance of line and its excess of cheap ornament. Any study of old bedroom furniture will make clear the inferiority of the modern manufacturer's designs. Nowhere is the old sense of proportion and fitness seen to better advantage than in the simple, admirably composed commodes and clothespresses of the eighteenth-century bedroom.

The bath-room walls and floor should, of course, be water-proof. In the average bath-room, a tiled floor and a high wainscoting of tiles are now usually seen; and the detached enamel or porcelain bath has in most cases replaced the built-in metal tub. The bath-rooms in the larger houses recently built are, in general, lined with marble; but though the use of this substance gives opportunity for fine architectural effects, few modern bath-rooms can in this respect be compared with those seen in the great houses of Europe. The chief fault of the American bath-room is that, however splendid the materials used, the treatment is seldom architectural. A glance at the beautiful bath-room in the Pitti Palace at Florence (see Plate LV) will show how much effect may be produced in a small space by carefully studied composition. A mere closet is here transformed into a stately room, by that regard for harmony of parts which distinguishes interior architecture from mere decoration. A bath-room lined with precious marbles, with bath and wash-stand ranged along the wall, regardless of their relation to the composition of the whole, is no better architecturally than the tiled bath-room seen in ordinary houses: design, not substance, is needed to make the one superior to the other.

XV

THE SCHOOL-ROOM AND NURSERIES

ONE of the most important and interesting problems in the planning and decoration of a house is that which has to do with the arrangement of the children's rooms.

There is, of course, little opportunity for actual decoration in school-room or nursery; and it is only by stretching a point that a book dealing merely with the practical application of æsthetics may be made to include a chapter bordering on pedagogy. It must be remembered, however, that any application of principles presupposes some acquaintance with the principles themselves; and from this standpoint there is a certain relevance in studying the means by which the child's surroundings may be made to develop his sense of beauty.

The room where the child's lessons are studied is, in more senses than one, that in which he receives his education. His whole view of what he is set to learn, and of the necessity and advantage of learning anything at all, is tinged, more often than people think, by the appearance of the room in which his studying is done. The æsthetic sensibilities wake early in some children, and these, if able to analyze their emotions, could testify to what suffering they have been subjected by the habit of sending to school-room and nurseries whatever furniture is too ugly or threadbare to be used in any other part of the house.

In the minds of such children, curious and lasting associations are early established between the appearance of certain rooms and the daily occupations connected with them; and the aspect of the school-room too often aggravates instead of mitigating the weariness of lesson-learning.

There are, of course, many children not naturally sensitive to artistic influences, and the parents of such children often think that no special care need be spent on their surroundings — a curious misconception of the purpose of all æsthetic training. To teach a child to appreciate any form of beauty is to develop his intelligence, and thereby to enlarge his capacity for wholesome enjoyment. It is, therefore, never idle to cultivate a child's taste; and those who have no pronounced natural bent toward the beautiful in any form need more guidance and encouragement than the child born with a sense of beauty. The latter will at most be momentarily offended by the sight of ugly objects; while they may forever blunt the taste and narrow the views of the child whose sluggish imagination needs the constant stimulus of beautiful surroundings.

If art is really a factor in civilization, it seems obvious that the feeling for beauty needs as careful cultivation as the other civic virtues. To teach a child to distinguish between a good and a bad painting, a well or an ill-modelled statue, need not hinder his growth in other directions, and will at least develop those habits of observation and comparison that are the base of all sound judgments. It is in this sense that the study of art is of service to those who have no special aptitude for any of its forms: its indirect action in shaping æsthetic criteria constitutes its chief value as an element of culture.

The habit of regarding "art" as a thing apart from life is fatal to the development of taste.   Parents may conscientiously send their children to galleries and museums, but unless the child can find some point of contact between its own surroundings and the contents of the galleries, the interest excited by the pictures and statues will be short-lived and ineffectual.   Children are not reached by abstract ideas, and a picture hanging on a museum wall is little better than an abstraction to the child's vivid but restricted imagination.   Besides, if the home surroundings are tasteless, the unawakened sense of form will not be roused by a hurried walk through a museum.   The child's mind must be prepared by daily lessons in beauty to understand the master-pieces of art.   A child brought up on foolish story-books could hardly be expected to enjoy *The Knight's Tale* or the *Morte d'Arthur* without some slight initiation into the nature and meaning of good literature; and to pass from a house full of ugly furniture, badly designed wall-papers and worthless knick-knacks to a hurried contemplation of the Venus of Milo or of a model of the Parthenon is not likely to produce the desired results.

The daily intercourse with poor pictures, trashy " ornaments," and badly designed furniture may, indeed, be fittingly compared with a mental diet of silly and ungrammatical story-books.   Most parents nowadays recognize the harmfulness of such a *régime*, and are careful to feed their children on more stimulating fare. Skilful compilers have placed Mallory and Chaucer, Cervantes and Froissart, within reach of the childish understanding, thus laying the foundations for a lasting appreciation of good literature. No greater service can be rendered to children than in teaching them to know the best and to want it; but while this is now generally conceded with regard to books, the child's eager eyes are left to fare as best they may on chromos from the illustrated papers and on carefully hoarded rubbish from the Christmas tree.

The mention of the Christmas tree suggests another obstacle to the early development of taste. Many children, besides being surrounded by ugly furniture and bad pictures, are overwhelmed at Christmas, and on every other anniversary, by presents not always selected with a view to the formation of taste. The question of presents is one of the most embarrassing problems in the artistic education of children. As long as they are in the toy age no great harm is done: it is when they are considered old enough to appreciate "something pretty for their rooms" that the season of danger begins. Parents themselves are often the worst offenders in this respect, and the sooner they begin to give their children presents which, if not beautiful, are at least useful, the sooner will the example be followed by relatives and friends. The selection of such presents, while it might necessitate a little more trouble, need not lead to greater expense. Good things do not always cost more than bad. A good print may often be bought for the same price as a poor one, and the money spent on a china "ornament," in the shape of a yellow Leghorn hat with a kitten climbing out of it, would probably purchase a good reproduction of one of the Tanagra statuettes, a plaster cast of some French or Italian bust, or one of Cantagalli's copies of the Robbia bas-reliefs — any of which would reveal a world of unsuspected beauty to many a child imprisoned in a circle of *articles de Paris.*

The children of the rich are usually the worst sufferers in such cases, since the presents received by those whose parents and relations are not "well off" have the saving merit of usefulness. It is the superfluous gimcrack—the "ornament"—which is most objectionable, and the more expensive such articles are the more likely are they to do harm. Rich children suffer from the quantity as well as the quality of the presents they receive. Appetite is surfeited, curiosity blunted, by the mass of offerings poured in with every anniversary. It would be better if, in such cases, friends and family could unite in giving to each child one thing worth having—a good edition, a first-state etching or engraving, or some like object fitted to give pleasure at the time and lasting enjoyment through life. Parents often make the mistake of thinking that such presents are too "serious"—that children do not care for good bindings, fine engravings, or reproductions of sculpture. As a matter of fact, children are quick to appreciate beauty when pointed out and explained to them, and an intelligent child feels peculiar pride in being the owner of some object which grown-up people would be glad to possess. If the selection of such presents is made with a reasonable regard for the child's tastes and understanding—if the book chosen is a good edition, well bound, of the *Morte d' Arthur* or of *Chaucer*—if the print represents some Tuscan Nativity, with a joyous dance of angels on the thatched roof, or a group of splendid horsemen and strange animals from the wondrous fairy-tale of the Riccardi chapel—the present will give as much immediate pleasure as a "juvenile" book or picture, while its intrinsic beauty and significance may become important factors in the child's æsthetic development. The possession of something valuable, that may not be knocked about, but must be handled with care and restored to its place after being looked at, will also cultivate in the child that habit of carefulness and order which may be defined as good manners toward inanimate objects.

Children suffer not only from the number of presents they receive, but from that over-crowding of modern rooms that so often makes it necessary to use the school-room and nurseries as an outlet for the overflow of the house. To the children's quarters come one by one the countless objects "too good to throw away" but too ugly to be tolerated by grown-up eyes — the bead-work cushions that have "associations," the mildewed Landseer prints of foaming, dying animals, the sheep-faced Madonna and Apostles in bituminous draperies, commemorating a paternal visit to Rome in the days when people bought copies of the "Old Masters."

Those who wish to train their children's taste must resolutely clear the school-room of all such stumbling-blocks. Ugly furniture cannot always be replaced; but it is at least possible to remove unsuitable pictures and knick-knacks.

It is essential that the school-room should be cheerful. Dark colors, besides necessitating the use of much artificial light, are depressing to children and consequently out of place in the school-room: white woodwork, and walls tinted in some bright color, form the best background for both work and play.

Perhaps the most interesting way of decorating the school-room is that which might be described as the rotation system. To carry out this plan — which requires the coöperation of the children's teacher — the walls must be tinted in some light color, such as turquoise-blue or pale green, and cleared of all miscellaneous adornments. These should then be replaced by a few carefully-chosen prints, photographs and plaster casts, representing objects connected with the children's studies. Let it, for instance, be supposed that the studies in hand include natural history, botany, and the history of France and England during the sixteenth century. These subjects might be respectively illustrated by some of the clever Japanese outline drawings of plants and animals, by

Holbein's portrait of Henry VIII, Clouet's of Charles IX and of Elizabeth of Austria, Dürer's etchings of Luther and Erasmus, and views of some of the principal buildings erected in France and England during the sixteenth century.

The prints and casts shown at one time should be sufficiently inexpensive and few in number to be changed as the child's lessons proceed, thus forming a kind of continuous commentary upon the various branches of study.

This plan of course necessitates more trouble and expense than the ordinary one of giving to the walls of the school-room a permanent decoration: an arrangement which may also be made interesting and suggestive, if the child's requirements are considered. When casts and pictures are intended to remain in place, it is a good idea to choose them at the outset with a view to the course of studies likely to be followed. In this way, each object may serve in turn to illustrate some phase of history or art: even this plan will be found to have a vivifying effect upon the dry bones of "lessons."

In a room decorated in this fashion, the prints or photographs selected might represent the foremost examples of Greek, Gothic, Renaissance and eighteenth-century architecture, together with several famous paintings of different periods and schools; sculpture being illustrated by casts of the Disk-thrower, of one of Robbia's friezes of child-musicians, of Donatello's Saint George, and Pigalle's "Child with the Bird."

Parents who do not care to plan the adornment of the school-room on such definite lines should at least be careful to choose appropriate casts and pictures. It is generally conceded that nothing painful should be put before a child's eyes; but the deleterious effects of namby-pamby prettiness are too often disregarded. Anything "sweet" is considered appropriate for the school-room or nursery; whereas it is essential to the child's artistic training that only the sweetness which proceeds *de forte* should be held up for admiration. It is easy to find among the world's masterpieces many pictures interesting to children. Vandyck's "Children of Charles I"; Bronzino's solemn portraits of Medici babies; Drouais' picture of the Comte d'Artois holding his little sister on the back of a goat; the wan little princes of Velasquez; the ruddy beggar-boys of Murillo — these are but a few of the subjects that at once suggest themselves. Then, again, there are the wonder-books of those greatest of all story-tellers, the Italian fresco-painters — Benozzo Gozzoli, Pinturicchio, Carpaccio — incorrigible gossips every one, lingering over the minor episodes and trivial details of their stories with the desultory slowness dear to childish listeners. In sculpture, the range of choice is no less extended. The choristers of Robbia, the lean little St. Johns of Donatello and his school — Verrocchio's fierce young David, and the Capitol "Boy with the Goose" — these may alternate with fragments of the Parthenon frieze, busts of great men, and studies of animals, from the Assyrian lions to those of Canova and Barye.

Above all, the walls should not be overcrowded. The importance of preserving in the school-room bare wall-spaces of uniform tint has hitherto been little considered; but teachers are beginning to understand the value of these spaces in communicating to the child's brain a sense of repose which diminishes mental and physical restlessness.

The furniture of the school-room should of course be plain and substantial. Well-designed furniture of this kind is seldom made by modern manufacturers, and those who can afford the slight

extra expense should commission a good cabinet-maker to reproduce some of the simple models which may be found in the
manuals of old French and English designers.   It is of special importance to provide a large, solid writing-table: children are too
often subjected to the needless constraint and fatigue of writing at
narrow unsteady desks, too small to hold even the books in use
during the lesson.

A well-designed bookcase with glass doors is a valuable factor
in the training of children.   It teaches a respect for books by showing that they are thought worthy of care; and a child is less likely
to knock about and damage a book which must be taken from
and restored to such a bookcase, than one which, after being
used, is thrust back on an open shelf.   Children's books, if they
have any literary value, should be bound in some bright-colored
morocco: dingy backs of calf or black cloth are not likely to attract the youthful eye, and the better a book is bound the more
carefully it will be handled.   Even lesson-books, when they become shabby, should have a covering of some bright-colored cloth
stitched over the boards.

The general rules laid down for the decoration of the school-
room may, with some obvious modifications, be applied to the
treatment of nursery and of children's rooms.   These, like the
school-room, should have painted walls and a floor of hard wood
with a removable rug or a square of matting.   In a house containing both school-room and nursery, the decoration of the latter
room will of course be adapted to the tastes of the younger children.   Mothers often say, in answer to suggestions as to the
decoration of the nursery, that little children "like something
bright"—as though this precluded every form of art above the
newspaper chromo and the Christmas card!   It is easy to pro-

duce an effect of brightness by means of white wood-work and walls hung with good colored prints, with large photographs of old Flemish or Italian pictures,—say, for example, Bellini's baby-angels playing on musical instruments,—and with a few of the Japanese plant and animal drawings already referred to.   All these subjects would interest and amuse even very young children; and there is no reason why a gay Japanese screen, with boldly drawn birds and flowers, should not afford as much entertainment as one composed of a heterogeneous collection of Christmas cards, chromos, and story-book pictures, put together without any attempt at color-harmony or composition.

Children's rooms should be as free as possible from all superfluous draperies.   The windows may be hung with either shades or curtains: it is needless to have both.   If curtains are preferred, they should be of chintz, or of some washable cotton or linen.   The reproductions of the old *toiles de Jouy*, with pictures from Æsop and La Fontaine, or from some familiar myth or story, are specially suited to children's rooms; while another source of interest and amusement may be provided by facing the fireplace with blue and white Dutch tiles representing the finding of Moses, the story of David and Goliath, or some such familiar episode.

As children grow older, and are allotted separate bedrooms, these should be furnished and decorated on the same principles and with the same care as the school-room.   Pieces of furniture for these bedrooms would make far more suitable and interesting presents than the costly odds and ends so often given without definite intention.   In the arrangement of the child's own room the expression of individual taste should be encouraged and the child allowed to choose the pictures and casts with which the walls are hung.   The responsibility of such selection will do much to develop the incipient faculties of observation and comparison.

To sum up, then : the child's visible surroundings form the basis of the best, because of the most unconscious, cultivation : and not of æsthetic cultivation only, since, as has been pointed out, the development of any artistic taste, if the child's general training is of the right sort, indirectly broadens the whole view of life.

XVI

BRIC-À-BRAC

IT is perhaps not uninstructive to note that we have no English word to describe the class of household ornaments which French speech has provided with at least three designations, each indicating a delicate and almost imperceptible gradation of quality. In place of bric-à-brac, bibelots, *objets d'art*, we have only knick-knacks—defined by Stormonth as "articles of small value."

This definition of the knick-knack fairly indicates the general level of our artistic competence. It has already been said that cheapness is not necessarily synonymous with trashiness; but hitherto this assertion has been made with regard to furniture and to the other necessary appointments of the house. With knick-knacks the case is different. An artistic age will of course produce any number of inexpensive trifles fit to become, like the Tanagra figurines, the museum treasures of later centuries; but it is hardly necessary to point out that modern shop-windows are not overflowing with such immortal toys. The few objects of art produced in the present day are the work of distinguished artists. Even allowing for what Symonds calls the "vicissitudes of taste," it seems improbable that our commercial knick-knack will ever be classed as a work of art.

It is clear that the weary man must have a chair to sit on, the hungry man a table to dine at; nor would the most sensitive judgment condemn him for buying ugly ones, were no others to be had; but objects of art are a counsel of perfection. It is quite possible to go without them; and the proof is that many do go without them who honestly think to possess them in abundance. This is said, not with any intention of turning to ridicule the natural desire to "make a room look pretty," but merely with the purpose of inquiring whether such an object is ever furthered by the indiscriminate amassing of "ornaments." Decorators know how much the simplicity and dignity of a good room are diminished by crowding it with useless trifles. Their absence improves even bad rooms, or makes them at least less multitudinously bad. It is surprising to note how the removal of an accumulation of knick-knacks will free the architectural lines and restore the furniture to its rightful relation with the walls.

Though a room must depend for its main beauty on design and furniture, it is obvious that there are many details of luxurious living not included in these essentials. In what, then, shall the ornamentation of rooms consist? Supposing walls and furniture to be satisfactory, how put the minor touches that give to a room the charm of completeness? To arrive at an answer, one must first consider the different kinds of minor embellishment. These may be divided into two classes: the object of art *per se*, such as the bust, the picture, or the vase; and, on the other hand, those articles, useful in themselves,—lamps, clocks, fire-screens, bookbindings, candelabra,—which art has only to touch to make them the best ornaments any room can contain. In past times such articles took the place of bibelots. Few purely ornamental objects were to be seen, save in the cabinets of collectors; but when Botticelli decorated the panels of linen chests, and Cellini chiselled book-clasps and drinking-cups, there could be no thought of the vicious distinction between the useful and the beautiful. One of the first obligations of art is to make all useful things beautiful: were this neglected principle applied to the manufacture of household accessories, the modern room would have no need of knick-knacks.

Before proceeding further, it is necessary to know what constitutes an object of art. It was said at the outset that, though cheapness and trashiness are not always synonymous, they are apt to be so in the case of the modern knick-knack. To buy, and even to make, it may cost a great deal of money; but artistically it is cheap, if not worthless; and too often its artistic value is in inverse ratio to its price. The one-dollar china pug is less harmful than an expensive onyx lamp-stand with moulded bronze mountings dipped in liquid gilding. It is one of the misfortunes of the present time that the most preposterously bad things often possess the powerful allurement of being expensive. One might think it an advantage that they are not within every one's reach; but, as a matter of fact, it is their very unattainableness which, by making them more desirable, leads to the production of that worst curse of modern civilization—cheap copies of costly horrors.

An ornament is of course not an object of art because it is expensive—though it must be owned that objects of art are seldom cheap. Good workmanship, as distinct from designing, almost always commands a higher price than bad; and good artistic workmanship having become so rare that there is practically no increase in the existing quantity of objects of art, it is evident that these are more likely to grow than to diminish in value. Still, as has been said, costliness is no test of merit in an age when large prices are paid for bad things. Perhaps the most convenient way of defining the real object of art is to describe it as *any ornamental object which adequately expresses an artistic conception.* This definition at least clears the ground of the mass of showy rubbish forming the stock-in-trade of the average " antiquity" dealer.

Good objects of art give to a room its crowning touch of distinction. Their intrinsic beauty is hardly more valuable than their suggestion of a mellower civilization—of days when rich men were patrons of " the arts of elegance," and when collecting beautiful objects was one of the obligations of a noble leisure. The qualities implied in the ownership of such bibelots are the mark of their unattainableness. The man who wishes to possess objects of art must have not only the means to acquire them, but the skill to choose them—a skill made up of cultivation and judgment, combined with that feeling for beauty that no amount of study can give, but that study alone can quicken and render profitable.

Only time and experience can acquaint one with those minor peculiarities marking the successive "manners" of a master, or even with the technical *nuances* which at once enable the collector to affix a date to his Sèvres or to his maiolica. Such knowledge is acquired at the cost of great pains and of frequent mistakes; but no one should venture to buy works of art who cannot at least draw such obvious distinctions as those between old and new Saxe, between an old Italian and a modern French bronze, or between Chinese peach-bloom porcelain of the Khang-hi period and the Japanese imitations to be found in every " Oriental emporium."

Supposing the amateur to have acquired this proficiency, he is still apt to buy too many things, or things out of proportion with the rooms for which they are intended. The scoffers at style— those who assume that to conform to any known laws of decoration is to sink one's individuality—often justify their view by the assertion that it is ridiculous to be tied down, in the choice of bibelots, to any given period or manner—as though Mazarin's great collection had comprised only seventeenth-century works of art, or the Colonnas, the Gonzagas, and the Malatestas had drawn all their treasures from contemporary sources! As a matter of fact, the great amateurs of the past were never fettered by such absurd restrictions. All famous patrons of art have encouraged the talent of their day; but the passion for collecting antiquities is at least as old as the Roman Empire, and Græco-Roman sculptors had to make archaistic statues to please the popular fancy, just as our artists paint pre-Raphaelite pictures to attract the disciples of Ruskin and William Morris. Since the Roman Empire, there has probably been no period when a taste for the best of all ages did not exist.[1] Julius II, while Michel Angelo and Raphael worked under his orders, was gathering antiques for the Belvedere *cortile;* under Louis XIV, Greek marbles, Roman bronzes, cabinets of Chinese lacquer and tables of Florentine mosaic were mingled without thought of discord against Lebrun's tapestries or Bérain's arabesques; and Marie-Antoinette's collection united Oriental porcelains with goldsmiths' work of the Italian Renaissance.

Taste attaches but two conditions to the use of objects of art:

[1] "A little study would probably show that the Ptolemaic era in Egypt was a renaissance of the Theban age, in architecture as in other respects, while the golden period of Augustus in Rome was largely a Greek revival. Perhaps it would even be discovered that all ages of healthy human prosperity are more or less revivals, and have been marked by a retrospective tendency." *The Architecture of the Renaissance in Italy,* by W. J. Anderson. London, Batsford, 1896.

that they shall be in scale with the room, and that the room shall
not be overcrowded with them.   There are two ways of being in
scale: there is the scale of proportion, and what might be called
the scale of appropriateness.   The former is a matter of actual
measurement, while the latter is regulated solely by the nicer
standard of good taste.   Even in the matter of actual measurement, the niceties of proportion are not always clear to an un-
practised eye.   It is easy to see that the Ludovisi Juno would be
out of scale in a boudoir, but the discrepancy, in diminishing,
naturally becomes less obvious.   Again, a vase or a bust may not
be out of scale with the wall-space behind it, but may appear to
crush the furniture upon which it stands; and since everything a
room contains should be regarded as a factor in its general composition, the relation of bric-à-brac to furniture is no less to be
studied than the relation of bric-à-brac to wall-spaces.   Much of
course depends upon the effect intended; and this can be greatly
modified by careful adjustment of the contents of the room.   A
ceiling may be made to look less high by the use of wide, low
pieces of furniture, with massive busts and vases; while a low-
studded room may be heightened by tall, narrow commodes and
cabinets, with objects of art upon the same general lines.

It is of no less importance to observe the scale of appropriateness.   A bronze Pallas Athene or a cowled mediæval *pleureur*
would be obviously out of harmony with the spirit of a boudoir;
while the delicate graces of old Saxe or Chelsea would become
futile in library or study.

Another kind of appropriateness must be considered in the relation of objects of art to each other: not only must they be in scale
as regards character and dimensions, but also — and this, though
more important, is perhaps less often considered — as regards

quality. The habit of mixing good, bad, and indifferent in furniture is often excused by necessity: people must use what they have. But there is no necessity for having bad bric-à-brac. Trashy " ornaments " do not make a room more comfortable; as a general rule, they distinctly diminish its comfort; and they have the further disadvantage of destroying the effect of any good piece of work. Vulgarity is always noisier than good breeding, and it is instructive to note how a modern commercial bronze will " talk down " a delicate Renaissance statuette or bust, and a piece of Deck or Minton china efface the color-values of blue-and-white or the soft tints of old Sèvres. Even those who set down a preference for old furniture as an affectation will hardly maintain that new knick-knacks are as good as old bibelots; but only those who have some slight acquaintance with the subject know how wide is the distance, in conception and execution, between the old object of art and its unworthy successor. Yet the explanation is simple. In former times, as the greatest painters occupied themselves with wall-decoration, so the greatest sculptors and modellers produced the delicate statuettes and the incomparable bronze mountings for vases and furniture adorning the apartments of their day. A glance into the window of the average furniture-shop probably convinces the most unobservant that modern bronze mountings are not usually designed by great artists; and there is the same change in the methods of execution. The bronze formerly chiselled is now moulded; the iron once wrought is cast; the patina given to bronze by a chemical process making it a part of the texture of the metal is now simply applied as a surface wash; and this deterioration in processes has done more than anything else to vulgarize modern ornament.

It may be argued that even in the golden age of art few could have walls decorated by great painters, or furniture-mountings modelled by great sculptors; but it is here that the superiority of the old method is shown. Below the great painter and sculptor came the trained designer who, formed in the same school as his superiors, did not attempt a poor copy of their masterpieces, but did the same kind of work on simpler lines; just as below the skilled artificer stood the plain artisan whose work was executed more rudely, but by the same genuine processes. This explains the supposed affectation of those who "like things just because they are old." Old bric-à-brac and furniture are, indeed, almost always worthy of liking, since they are made on good lines by a good process.

Two causes connected with the change in processes have contributed to the debasement of bibelots: the substitution of machine for hand-work has made possible the unlimited reproduction of works of art; and the resulting demand for cheap knick-knacks has given employment to a multitude of untrained designers having nothing in common with the *virtuoso* of former times.

It is an open question how much the mere possibility of unlimited reproduction detracts from the intrinsic value of an object of art. To the art-lover, as distinguished from the collector, uniqueness *per se* can give no value to an inartistic object; but the distinction, the personal quality, of a beautiful object is certainly enhanced when it is known to be alone of its kind — as in the case of the old bronzes made *à cire perdue*. It must, however, be noted that in some cases — as in that of bronze-casting — the method which permits reproduction is distinctly inferior to that used when but one object is to be produced.

In writing on objects of art, it is difficult to escape the charge of saying on one page that reproductions are objectionable, and on the next that they are better than poor "originals." The United States customs laws have drawn a rough distinction between an original work and its reproductions, defining the former as a work of art and the latter as articles of commerce; but it does not follow that an article of commerce may not be an adequate representation of a work of art. The technical differences incidental to the various forms of reproduction make any general conclusion impossible. In the case of bronzes, for instance, it has been pointed out that the *cire perdue* process is superior to that by means of which reproductions may be made; nor is this the only cause of inferiority in bronze reproductions. The nature of bronze-casting makes it needful that the final touches should be given to bust or statue after it emerges from the mould. Upon these touches, given by the master's chisel, the expressiveness and significance of the work chiefly depend; and multiplied reproductions, in lacking this individual stamp, must lack precisely that which distinguishes the work of art from the commercial article.

Perhaps the safest general rule is to say that the less the reproduction suggests an attempt at artistic interpretation,—the more literal and mechanical is its rendering of the original,—the better it fulfils its purpose. Thus, plaster-casts of sculpture are more satisfactory than bronze or marble copies; and a good photograph of a painting is superior to the average reproduction in oils or water-color.

The deterioration in gilding is one of the most striking examples of the modern disregard of quality and execution. In former times gilding was regarded as one of the crowning touches of magnificence in decoration, was little used except where great splendor of effect was desired, and was then applied by means of a difficult and costly process. To-day, after a period of reaction during which all gilding was avoided, it is again unsparingly used, under the mistaken impression that it is one of the chief characteristics of the French styles now once more in demand. The result is a plague of liquid gilding. Even in France, where good gilding is still done, the great demand for cheap gilt furniture and ornaments has led to the general use of the inferior process. The prevalence of liquid gilding, and the application of gold to furniture and decoration not adapted to such treatment, doubtless explain the aversion of many persons to any use of gilding in decoration.

In former times the expense of good gilding was no obstacle to its use, since it was employed only in gala rooms, where the whole treatment was on the same scale of costliness: it would never have occurred to the owner of an average-sized house to drench his walls and furniture in gilding, since the excessive use of gold in decoration was held to be quite unsuited to such a purpose. Nothing more surely preserves any form of ornament from vulgarization than a general sense of fitness.

Much of the beauty and propriety of old decoration was due to the fact that the merit of a work of art was held to consist, not in substance, but in design and execution. It was never thought that a badly designed bust or vase could be saved from mediocrity by being made of an expensive material. Suitability of substance always enhances a work of art; mere costliness never. The chryselephantine Zeus of Olympia was doubtless admirably suited to the splendor of its surroundings; but in a different setting it would have been as beautiful in marble. In plastic art everything depends on form and execution, and the skilful handling of a substance deliberately chosen for its resistance (where another might have been used with equal fitness) is rather a *tour de force* than an artistic achievement.

These last generalizations are intended to show, not only that there is an intrinsic value in almost all old bibelots, but also that the general excellence of design and execution in past times has handed down to us many unimportant trifles in the way of furniture and household appliances worthy of being regarded as minor objects of art.   In Italy especially, where every artisan seems to have had the gift of the *plasticatore* in his finger-tips, and no substance was thought too poor to express a good design, there are still to be found many bits of old workmanship — clocks, *appliques*, terra-cottas, and carved picture-frames with touches of gilding — that may be characterized in the terms applied by the builder of Buckingham House to his collection of pictures: — "Some good, *none disagreeable.*"   Still, no accumulation of such trifles, even where none is disagreeable, will give to a room the same distinction as the presence of a few really fine works of art.   Any one who has the patience to put up with that look of bareness so displeasing to some will do better to buy each year one superior piece rather than a dozen of middling quality.

Even the buyer who need consult only his own pleasure must remember that his very freedom from the ordinary restrictions lays him open to temptation.   It is no longer likely that any collector will be embarrassed by a superfluity of treasures; but he may put too many things into one room, and no amount of individual merit in the objects themselves will, from the decorator's standpoint, quite warrant this mistake.   Any work of art, regardless of its intrinsic merit, must justify its presence in a room by being *more valuable than the space it occupies* — more valuable, that is, to the general scheme of decoration.

Those who call this view arbitrary or pedantic should consider, first, the importance of plain surfaces in decoration, and secondly the tendency of overcrowding to minimize the effect of each separate object, however striking in itself. Eye and mind are limited in their receptivity to a certain number of simultaneous impressions, and the Oriental habit of displaying only one or two objects of art at a time shows a more delicate sense of these limitations than the Western passion for multiplying effects.

To sum up, then, a room should depend for its adornment on general harmony of parts, and on the artistic quality of such necessities as lamps, screens, bindings, and furniture. Whoever goes beyond these essentials should limit himself in the choice of ornaments to the "labors of the master-artist's hand."

CONCLUSION

IN the preceding pages an attempt has been made to show that in the treatment of rooms we have passed from the golden age of architecture to the gilded age of decoration.

Any argument in support of a special claim necessitates certain apparent injustices, sets up certain provisional limitations, and can therefore be judged with fairness only by those who make due allowance for these conditions. In the discussion of æsthetics such impartiality can seldom be expected. Not unnaturally, people resent any attempt to dogmatize on matters so generally thought to lie within the domain of individual judgment. Many hold that in questions of taste *Gefühl ist alles;* while those who believe that beyond the oscillations of fashion certain fixed laws may be discerned have as yet agreed upon no formula defining their belief. In short, our civilization has not yet developed any artistic creed so generally recognized that it may be invoked on both sides of an argument without risk of misunderstanding.

This is true at least of those forms of art that minister only to the æsthetic sense. With architecture and its allied branches the case is different. Here beauty depends on fitness, and the practical requirements of life are the ultimate test of fitness.

If, therefore, it can be proved that the old practice was based upon a clearer perception of these requirements than is shown by modern decorators, it may be claimed not unreasonably that the old methods are better than the new. It seems, however, that the distinction between the various offices of art is no longer clearly recognized. The merit of house-decoration is now seldom measured by the standard of practical fitness; and those who would set up such a standard are suspected of proclaiming individual preferences under the guise of general principles.

In this book, an endeavor has been made to draw no conclusion unwarranted by the premises; but whatever may be thought of the soundness of some of the deductions, they must be regarded, not as a criticism of individual work, but simply of certain tendencies in modern architecture. It must be remembered, too, that the book is merely a sketch, intended to indicate the lines along which further study may profitably advance.

It may seem inconsequent that an elementary work should include much apparently unimportant detail. To pass in a single chapter from a discussion of abstract architectural laws to the combination of colors in a bedroom carpet seems to show lack of plan; yet the transition is logically justified. In the composition of a whole there is no negligible quantity: if the decoration of a room is planned on certain definite principles, whatever contributes line or color becomes a factor in the composition. The relation of proportion to decoration is like that of anatomy to sculpture : underneath are the everlasting laws. It was the recognition of this principle that kept the work of the old architect-decorators (for the two were one) free from the superfluous, free from the intemperate accumulation that marks so many modern rooms. Where each detail had its determinate part, no superficial accessories were needed to make up a whole: a great draughtsman represents with a few strokes what lesser artists can express only by a multiplicity of lines.

The supreme excellence is simplicity. Moderation, fitness, relevance — these are the qualities that give permanence to the work of the great architects. *Tout ce qui n'est pas nécessaire est nuisible.* There is a sense in which works of art may be said to endure by virtue of that which is left out of them, and it is this "tact of omission" that characterizes the master-hand.

Modern civilization has been called a varnished barbarism: a definition that might well be applied to the superficial graces of much modern decoration. Only a return to architectural principles can raise the decoration of houses to the level of the past. Vasari said of the Farnesina palace that it was not built, but really born — *non murato ma veramente nato ;* and this phrase is but the expression of an ever-present sense — the sense of interrelation of parts, of unity of the whole.

There is no absolute perfection, there is no communicable ideal; but much that is empiric, much that is confused and extravagant, will give way before the application of principles based on common sense and regulated by the laws of harmony and proportion.

INDEX

A PORTFOLIO OF PICTURES OF
INTERIORS AND DETAILS/Done
According to the Canon of *The Decoration
of Houses*

Three Phases of Codman's Style

LVII A SALON AT "LA LÉOPOLDA"

WITH CORNICES AND PAINTED DECORATIONS IN THE LOUIS XVI
STYLE

Society for the Preservation of New England Antiquities

LVII B MUSIC ROOM AT DUMBARTON OAKS

WASHINGTON, D.C.

WITH RENAISSANCE CEILING, MANTEL, AND TAPESTRIES

The Dumbarton Oaks Collection

**LVIII   A CHARACTERISTIC CODMAN ENTRANCE
HALL AT 7 EAST 96TH STREET, NEW YORK**

The Metropolitan Museum of Art, Gift of the Estate of Ogden Codman, Jr., 1951

Ogden Codman's Plans
for Newport

**LIX WALL IN THE LOUIS XVI STYLE FOR "THE
BREAKERS" (DETAIL)**

The Metropolitan Museum of Art, Gift of the Estate of Ogden Codman, Jr., 1951

**LX A   MANTEL, MIRROR, DOORS, AND SCONCES
IN THE LOUIS XV STYLE FOR
CHÂTEAU-SUR-MER, THE RESIDENCE OF G. P.
WETMORE**

The Metropolitan Museum of Art, Gift of the Estate of Ogden Codman, Jr., 1951

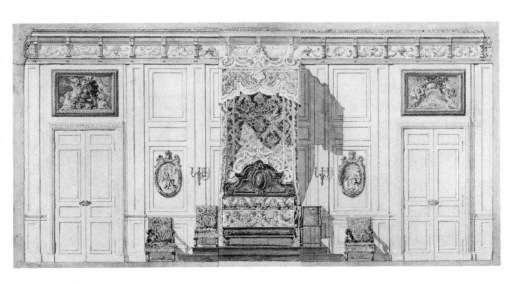

**LX B   CANOPIED BED AND ACCOMPANYING
DETAILS FOR "THE BREAKERS"**

The Metropolitan Museum of Art, Gift of the Estate of Ogden Codman, Jr., 1951

Two Early Disciples: Elsie de Wolfe and F. Burrall Hoffman

LXI   VILLA TRIANON

VERSAILLES

(DECORATED BY ELSIE DE WOLFE, LADY MENDL)

Jerome Zerbe

LXII   DETAIL OF "VIZCAYA"

MIAMI

(F. BURRALL HOFFMAN JR., ARCHITECT)

John Barrington Bayley

An Horace Trumbauer Portfolio

LXIII DRAWING ROOM OF "MIRAMAR,"
RESIDENCE OF DR. ALEXANDER H. RICE

NEWPORT

Tebbs-Knell Photo; Collection of Alfred Branam, Jr.

LXIV A BEDROOM AT "WHITEMARSH," RESIDENCE OF E. T. STOTESBURY

PHILADELPHIA

Mattie E. Hewitt; Collection of Alfred Branam, Jr.

LXIV B DETAIL OF BALLROOM, "WHITEMARSH"

Mattie E. Hewitt; Collection of Alfred Branam, Jr.

The Grand Entrance Hall
in Trumbauer's Manner

LXV   "ROSE TERRACE," THE RESIDENCE OF MRS.
HORACE DODGE

GROSSE POINTE FARMS, MICHIGAN

Frederick Miller; Collection of Alfred Branam, Jr.

LXVI ENTRANCE TO WILDENSTEIN & CO., INC.

NEW YORK

Classical Rooms in the Great
New York Clubs
(McKIM, MEAD, AND WHITE)

LXVII   SITTING ROOM

THE UNIVERSITY CLUB

John Barrington Bayley

LXVIII SALON

THE METROPOLITAN CLUB

John Barrington Bayley

Allyn Cox, American Muralist

**LXIX MURALS BY ALLYN COX AT THE WILLIAM
ANDREWS CLARK, JR., MEMORIAL LIBRARY**

THE UNIVERSITY OF CALIFORNIA AT LOS ANGELES (CA. 1924–26)

(ROBERT D. FARQUHAR, ARCHITECT)

Hiller Photo; Courtesy Allyn Cox

LXX A   A COX MURAL AT THE
CALHOUN-THORNWELL HOUSE

ATLANTA

(PHILIP TRAMMELL SHUTZE, ARCHITECT)

Atlanta Historical Society

LXX B   DETAIL OF MURALS BY ALLYN COX IN
THE CLARK MEMORIAL LIBRARY

Henry Hope Reed

LXXI MANTEL, METROPOLITAN CLUB

NEW YORK CITY

(McKIM, MEAD, AND WHITE)

John Barrington Bayley

Gesso and Ormolu

LXXII   BENCH, GREENWICH SAVINGS BANK
36TH STREET AND BROADWAY, NEW YORK CITY
(DESIGNED BY YORK AND SAWYER)
John Barrington Bayley

Bookcase and Fireplace

**LXXIII   PROPOSAL FOR BOOKCASE BY OGDEN
CODMAN, JR.**

The Metropolitan Museum of Art, Gift of the Estate of Ogden Codman, Jr., 1951

LXXIV   MANTEL IN DRAWING ROOM OF
"BARBADOS HILL"

DEVON, PENNSYLVANIA

(BY HORACE TRUMBAUER)

John Barrington Bayley

Classical Foyer and Bathroom

LXXV   UNIVERSITY CLUB

NEW YORK CITY.

(McKIM, MEAD, AND WHITE)

John Barrington Bayley

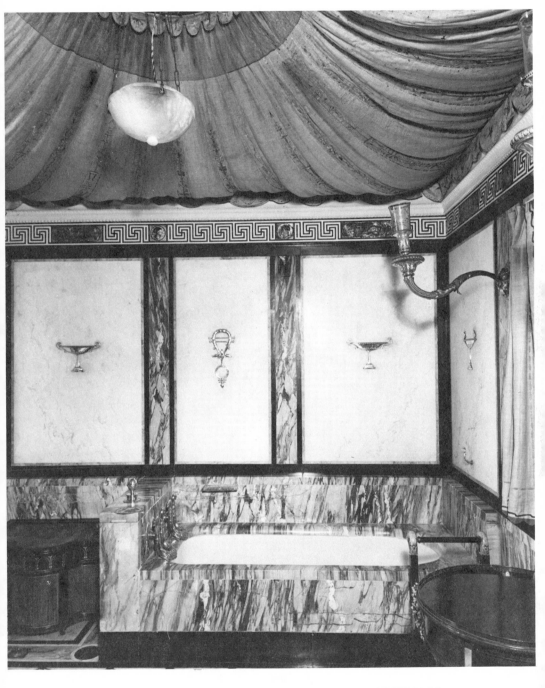

LXXVI "VIZCAYA," BATHROOM WITH GRECIAN
DECORATIONS

(F. BURRALL HOFFMAN, JR., ARCHITECT; PAUL CHALFIN,
DECORATOR)

Miami-Metro Department of Publicity and Tourism

Classical Details, ca. 1915 and ca. 1970

**LXXVII   JEAN-LOUIS BOURGEOIS, SKETCH FOR A
CARTOUCHE, SAN FRANCISCO 1915 EXPOSITION,
PALACE OF HORTICULTURE**

Arthur Brown, Jr., Collection, San Francisco

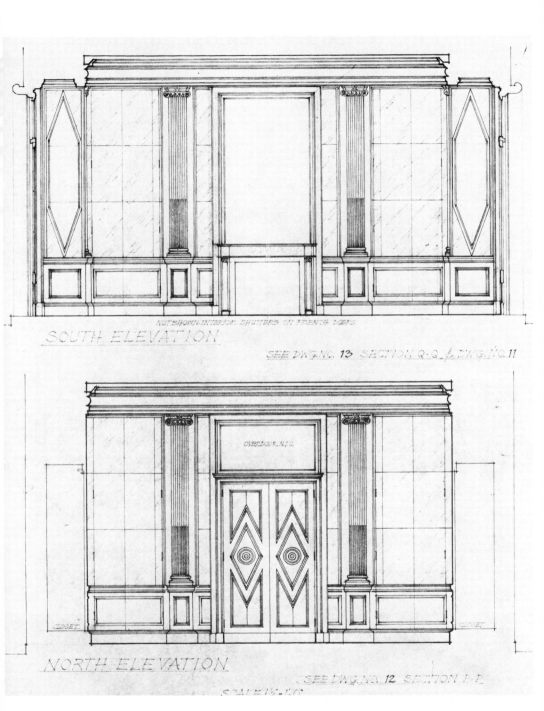

SOUTH ELEVATION

NOT SHOWN INTERIOR SHUTTERS ON FRENCH DOORS

SEE DWG.NO. 13 SECTION Q-Q & DWG.NO. 11

OVERDOOR. N.I.C.

CLOSET

CLOSET

NORTH ELEVATION

SEE DWG.NO. 12 SECTION P-P

SCALE 3/4" = 1'-0"

LXXVIII   JOHN BARRINGTON BAYLEY, DETAIL
OF INTERIOR, PROPOSED EDWARD DINSHA
HOUSE

John Barrington Bayley

The Scaled-Down and Simplified
Taste of the Twenties
and Thirties

LXXIX DINING ROOM OF THE HOGAN-CURTIS
HOUSE, MACON, GEORGIA

(PHILIP TRAMMELL SHUTZE, ARCHITECT; DAVID R. BYERS III,
DECORATOR)

Helga Photo Studio, Inc.

LXXX A ENTRANCE HALL TO THE SWAN HOUSE, ATLANTA HISTORICAL SOCIETY

(BY PHILIP TRAMMELL SHUTZE, ARCHITECT)

Atlanta Historical Society

LXXX B LIBRARY, 2300 FOXHALL ROAD, WASHINGTON, RESIDENCE OF THE BELGIAN AMBASSADOR

(BY HORACE TRUMBAUER)

Collection of Alfred Branam, Jr.